Advanced Introduction to Organis

Elgar Advanced Introductions are stimulating and thoughtful introductions to major fields in the social sciences and law, expertly written by the world's leading scholars. Designed to be accessible yet rigorous, they offer concise and lucid surveys of the substantive and policy issues associated with discrete subject areas.

The aims of the series are two-fold: to pinpoint essential principles of a particular field, and to offer insights that stimulate critical thinking. By distilling the vast and often technical corpus of information on the subject into a concise and meaningful form, the books serve as accessible introductions for undergraduate and graduate students coming to the subject for the first time. Importantly, they also develop well-informed, nuanced critiques of the field that will challenge and extend the understanding of advanced students, scholars and policy-makers.

For a full list of titles in the series please see the back of the book. Recent titles in the series include:

Post Keynesian Economics
J.E. King

International Intellectual Property
Susy Frankel and Daniel J. Gervais

Public Management and
Administration
Christopher Pollitt

Organised Crime
Leslie Holmes

The Law of International
Organizations
Jan Klabbers

International Environmental Law
Ellen Hey

International Sales Law
Clayton P. Gillette

Advanced Introduction to

Organised Crime

LESLIE HOLMES

*Professor Emeritus of Political Science, University of Melbourne, Australia
and Recurrent Visiting Professor, University of Bologna, Italy, Graduate
School for Social Research, Warsaw, Poland and People's University,
Beijing, China*

Elgar Advanced Introductions

Edward Elgar
PUBLISHING

Cheltenham, UK • Northampton, MA, USA

Published by
Edward Elgar Publishing Limited
The Lypiatts
15 Lansdown Road
Cheltenham
Glos GL50 2JA
UK

Edward Elgar Publishing, Inc.
William Pratt House
9 Dewey Court
Northampton
Massachusetts 01060
USA

A catalogue record for this book
is available from the British Library

Library of Congress Control Number: 2015957865

MIX
Paper from
responsible sources
FSC
www.fsc.org   FSC® C013056

ISBN 978 1 78347 194 2 (cased)
ISBN 978 1 78347 195 9 (paperback)
ISBN 978 1 78347 196 6 (eBook)

Typeset by Servis Filmsetting Ltd, Stockport, Cheshire
Printed and bound in Great Britain by TJ International Ltd, Padstow

For Mei Nu, Minister of Culture

Contents

Preface

Although it has existed throughout history and in all parts of the world, it is only in the past three decades that the threat from and impact of organised crime (OC) has begun to be properly acknowledged. One major reason for this is that OC has become increasingly transnational since the 1990s. The first truly global treaty against OC, that of the UN, dates only from 2000, and entered into force as recently as September 2003.

Although this book introduces readers to all forms of OC and transnational organised crime (TOC) and in all parts of the world, there is a particular focus on a specific aspect of OC activity, namely trafficking in human beings (THB). There is also more emphasis on Europe and Asia than on other parts of the world.

The clandestine nature of most OC activity and the dangers involved in researching it make it difficult to provide scholarly analysis of some aspects of it. Where possible, serious academic works have been the primary source of the material in this book. But there are often times when it is both necessary and desirable to use alternative sources, such as official reports and analyses by investigative journalists. As an academic myself, subject to my university's stringent research ethics requirements, I am aware that journalists can sometimes go where academics have been forbidden to venture; I am both grateful to and often envious of such journalists.

Many analysts distinguish what they call mafia-style organisations from other forms of OC; given this, such organisations are here called mafias (that is, lower case), while the Sicilian original version is called the Mafia. A second terminological clarification is that a number of agencies nowadays prefer to use the label "serious and organised crime", rather than simply "organised crime". They do this in recognition of the fact that the highly structured and code-based gangs that many people still envisage when they see the term "organised crime" are being superseded by much more flexible and transient groups; the descriptor "organised" is potentially misleading for the latter. After deliberation, it was decided to adhere to the term "organised crime" for this study. One reason is that it is still far more familiar to most people; rather than replace it, our preference is to explain how it is currently changing its nature and meaning in significant ways. A second reason is that "serious crime" can refer to activities that fall well outside the purview of this book, such as crimes of passion resulting in death or serious injury.

I wish to thank my students in Bologna (Forlì), Melbourne and Warsaw, who have been subjected to many aspects of this book via seminars in recent years, and who have provided me with invaluable feedback and information. At Edward Elgar, I thank Harry Fabian, Vicki Litherland, Emily Mew, Tori Nicols and Alexandra O'Connell for their tolerance, encouragement and good humour.

Finally, I extend particular thanks to my wife Becky for being so understanding and supportive when I spend far longer in my study and on work-related overseas trips than I should.

Leslie Holmes
Melbourne
September 2015

Acronyms

ACOSS	Australian Council of Social Service
AI	Amnesty International
AMA	American Motorcyclist Association
AML	Anti-Money Laundering
APEC	Asia-Pacific Economic Cooperation
ASEAN	Association of Southeast Asian Nations
ATM	Automated Teller Machine
CCTV	Closed Circuit Television
CD	Compact Disc
CEE	Central and Eastern Europe
CIA	Central Intelligence Agency
COCI	Composite Organized Crime Index
CoE	Council of Europe
CPI	Corruption Perceptions Index
DEA	Drug Enforcement Administration
DPJ	Democratic Party of Japan
DVD	Digital Video (or Versatile) Disc
EC3	European Cybercrime Centre
FARC	Revolutionary Armed Forces of Colombia
FATF	Financial Action Task Force
FBI	Federal Bureau of Investigation
FSI	Fragile States Index *or* Financial Secrecy Index
FSU	Former Soviet Union
GCR	Global Competitiveness Report
GFC	Global Financial Crisis
GRETA	Group of Experts on Action against Trafficking in Human Beings
HIV	Human Immunodeficiency Virus
ICIJ	International Consortium of Investigative Journalists
ICVS	International Crime Victim Survey
ILO	International Labour Organization
INGO	International Non-Governmental Organisation
IO	International Organisation

IOM	International Organization for Migration
IP	Intellectual Property
IS	Islamic State
KGB	(Russian for) Committee for State Security
LCN	La Cosa Nostra
Mercosur	Mercado Común del Sur (Common Market of the South)
MS	member state(s)
NAFTA	North American Free Trade Agreement
NCA	National Crime Agency
NCPC	National Crime Prevention Council
NGO	Non-Governmental Organisation
OC	Organised Crime
OCG	Organised Crime Group
OECD	Organisation for Economic Co-operation and Development
OMCG	Outlaw Motor Cycle Gang
OSCE	Organization for Security and Co-operation in Europe
PACO	Programme Against Corruption and Organised Crime in South-eastern Europe
RCT	Rational Choice Theory
SCO	Shanghai Cooperation Organisation
SEE	South Eastern Europe
STD	Sexually Transmitted Disease
THB	Trafficking in Human Beings
TiP	Trafficking in Persons
TJN	Tax Justice Network
TNGO	Transnational Non-Governmental Organisation
TOC	Transnational Organised Crime
UN	United Nations
UNAMA	United Nations Assistance Mission in Afghanistan
UNCTOC	UN Convention against Transnational Organized Crime
UNODC	United Nations Office on Drugs and Crime
USSR	Union of Soviet Socialist Republics
WTO	World Trade Organization

1 Definitional aspects

The concept of organised crime (OC) is nothing new, with some of its Asian and European variants having been traced back to the seventeenth century (Fijnaut 2014); it will be shown below that some activities that can legitimately be called OC can be traced back even earlier. However, it is widely – if not universally – accepted that it has become an increasingly serious security problem for states and societies worldwide since the late-twentieth century. This is to no small extent because, in the era of globalisation, OC has become increasingly *transnational*, so that we now often refer to transnational organised crime or TOC. This is a relatively new term. In the 1970s, the UN's Crime Prevention and Criminal Justice Branch coined the term "transnational crime" (Wright 2006: 22) while, as Siegel and Nelen (2008: 1) point out, it was not until the mid-1990s that the term "global organised crime" came into use. Even the term organised crime is *relatively* new: Klaus von Lampe (2001: 99) notes that it was first coined in Chicago in 1919, so it has only been in use for less than a century.

But what exactly do we mean when we refer to "organised crime"? While we all might have an image in our minds when we hear these words, can we be certain that we have essentially the *same* image? Evidently we do not, and this chapter highlights many of the reasons for the existence of so many differing conceptions of the term.

To convey some idea of the range of views, it is worth noting that leading New York-based German criminologist Klaus von Lampe has identified some 180 definitions of OC, indicative of the wide range of views on this.[1] This chapter begins with a very brief history of OC, and then examines the definitions provided by various "official" institutions, both international and in individual states, before considering some of the best-known academic definitions. Following this, some of the principal differences between OC and closely related concepts are elaborated, and the range of activities in which OC engages is listed, before drawing conclusions.

1

1.1   Organised crime in historical perspective

As noted above, OC is not a new phenomenon. Many readers will think of Chicago in the 1920s and the Al Capone gang as an early example of OC, but there is evidence of this type of criminality much earlier. For instance, the Sicilian mafia dates from the early nineteenth century, while Albanian OC has existed since at least the sixteenth century. But OC has been traced back much further to ancient Rome and ancient Greece, with early "godfathers" such as Clodius and Milo in the former, and OC in the latter being compared with the Sicilian Mafia (Wees 1999; but see Fisher 1999 for an argument that the scale of OC in ancient Greece may have been smaller than usually assumed); there is also evidence of OC in the Ottoman Empire (Gingeras 2014: 21–2). Indeed, in a controversial but thought-provoking analysis, Charles Tilly (1985) – developing the argument made by Saint Augustine in his fifth century work *City of God* that states are merely "large bandit bands" – argues that the modern state has its origins in a particular form of OC activity involving extortion for the purposes of war-making (namely, violence).

There are some important differences between most earlier forms of OC and what has emerged in the past hundred years or so, however. For instance, there is far less piracy and highway banditry nowadays than in the past, though Somali piracy in the 2000s demonstrates that this form of OC activity has not completely disappeared. This said, analysts such as Paul Lunde (2004) have noted important similarities between invading forces in past centuries and twentieth century (T)OC; these include that both are mostly non-ideological, use or threaten violent means, and observe their own codes rather than those of areas in which they are operating.

1.2   Institutional definitions

OC activity is also known as racketeering, while members of OC groups are often called gangsters, mobsters or hoods. But simply providing synonyms does not tell us what OC is, so that we need to consider actual definitions.

Probably the most frequently cited institutional definition of OC is that provided in the United Nation's (UN's) Convention against

Transnational Organized Crime (UNCTOC), which was adopted in Palermo – a symbolic location, given that Sicily is the Mafia's home base – in 2000. This Convention provides the following definitions of various concepts relating to organised crime:

- "Organised criminal group" shall mean a structured group of three or more persons, existing for a period of time and acting in concert with the aim of committing one or more serious crimes or offences established in accordance with this Convention, in order to obtain, directly or indirectly, a financial or other material benefit;
- "Serious crime" shall mean conduct constituting an offence punishable by a maximum deprivation of liberty of at least four years or a more serious penalty;
- "Structured group" shall mean a group that is not randomly formed for the immediate commission of an offence and that does not need to have formally defined roles for its members, continuity of its membership or a developed structure (UNODC 2004: 5).

In 2008, the Council of the European Union adopted its own definition, which was heavily influenced by the UN's definition (Council of the European Union 2008: Article 1.1). But more than a decade earlier, in April 1997, the EU had provided a list of criteria to be met in order for an act to be considered an act of organised crime; *at least six* of the following eleven characteristics had to be present, and four of them had to be those numbered 1, 3, 5 and 11 (bolded):

1. **Collaboration of more than two people**
2. each with their own appointed tasks
3. **for a prolonged or indefinite period of time** (this criterion refers to the stability and [potential] durability of the group)
4. using some form of discipline and control
5. **suspected of the commission of serious criminal offences**
6. operating on an international level
7. using violence or other means suitable for intimidation
8. using commercial or businesslike structures
9. engaged in money laundering
10. exerting influence on politics, the media, public administration, judicial authorities or the economy
11. **motivated by the pursuit of profit and/or power.** (cited in Vander Beken et al. 2006: 50)

More recently, Bąkowski (2013a: 2) has argued that one of the problems within the EU is that there are *three* basic approaches to OC in the national criminal legislation of member states:

- The civil law approach, which criminalises participation in a criminal association.
- The common law approach, which is based on the notion of conspiracy, that is, an agreement to commit a crime.
- The Scandinavian approach, which rejects the notion of "criminal organisation" offences and instead relies on the application of general criminal law, such as complicity, or aiding and abetting.

Clearly, if there is such a variety of approaches in an organisation that has for decades been seeking standardisation across a wide range of issues, the problems of reaching universal agreement on a definition are substantial. The scope of this problem is further emphasised by Bąkowski (2013a: 2) when he points out that even *within* these three approaches there can be significant diversity. Thus the Italian (civil law) definition of mafia-type groupings is quite different from that in many other civil law jurisdictions. For these and other reasons, and in an officially sanctioned EU document, he argues that the 2008 attempt by the EU to formulate a common definition of OC "has been widely considered a failure" (Bąkowski 2013a: 1).

Since many readers will be UK-based, it is worth noting the official definition of OC provided by the new (operational since October 2013, and replacing the Serious Organised Crime Agency) National Crime Agency (NCA). Nowadays, the British authorities prefer to use a slightly longer term than many academics and other agencies use, namely "Serious and organised crime", since they wish to include in their analyses and policies serious crimes committed by individuals or pairs of individuals cooperating in loose networks as well as by the "three or more" people required in most official international approaches for classification as an OC group (OCG). Thus the NCA (2014: 7), citing the UK Government's Strategy, defines "serious and organised crime" as:

> serious crime planned, co-ordinated and conducted by people working together on a continuing basis. Their motivation is often, but not always, financial gain . . . . Organised crime in this and other countries recognises neither national borders nor national interests . . . . Generally, serious and organised crime . . . operates in loose networks where individuals, pairs or

small groups bring associates and contacts together to work on particular enterprises across multiple crime types. Some serious and organised crime is perpetrated by hierarchically structured groups comprising close associates and/or family members, some of whom are based overseas.

This detailed definition has replaced the earlier definition favoured by the National Crime Intelligence Service that operated in the UK from 1992 to 2002, according to which organised crime comprises "Any enterprise or group of persons engaged in continuing illegal activities which has as its primary purpose the generation of profit irrespective of national boundaries" (cited in Hobbs and Hobbs 2012: 258). While the latest definition is long, it is also more nuanced than earlier approaches, and conveys well the considerable variety of ways in which contemporary OC may operate and be structured. Indeed, not only is it more nuanced, but it does actually define the term organised crime; observant readers will have noticed that the definitions provided by the UN and the EU define various terms closely connected to OC, but not the term itself.

Finally, we can cite the FBI's definition of an OCG, which is shorter and in some ways punchier than those already considered:

> any group having some manner of a formalized structure and whose primary objective is to obtain money through illegal activities. Such groups maintain their position through the use of actual or threatened violence, corrupt public officials, graft, or extortion, and generally have a significant impact on the people in their locales, region, or the country as a whole. (FBI 2015)

This is a reasonable definition, but the reference to a "formalized structure" means that it does not overtly include some of the newer, much looser network forms of OC; while the use of the phrase "some manner of" might allow for these looser forms, the NCA definition, though wordier, does so more explicitly. It could be objected that if structures are very loose, then we should not use the term *organised* anyway. While there is some validity to this point, the fact that such groups are involved in many of the same types of activity in which more structured groupings engage is one good reason why both types of gang should be included under the rubric of OC.

1.3   Academic definitions

Unfortunately, there is even more disagreement among academic specialists on what constitutes OC than there is among states and IOs (for a critical outline of the key debates see Paoli and Vander Beken 2014). A selection of the most frequently cited endorses this point.

Three of the best-known approaches from the late-1960s and early-1970s are those of Donald Cressey, Joseph Albini and Thomas Schelling. Cressey (1967: 29), who has been described as "the founder of the modern study of organized crime" (Organized Crime Research 2015), distinguishes between ordinary criminals and organised criminals, arguing that while the former are exclusively predatory, the latter do offer something – illicit goods or services – to those members of the public wanting them. As we shall see below, this is not a fully convincing or universally applicable distinction, however.

Albini (1971) argued that criminal groups should not be classified in terms of the group's characteristics (for example, its ethnic composition or structure), but rather in terms of the type of criminal activities in which it engages. This revealed real prescience: as he rightly noted almost half a century ago, long before criminal groups had become as fluid as so many of them have in the past 25 years or so, criminal groups are dynamic, and mutate according to changes in market supply and demand, anti-crime policies, and other factors considered later in this book.

Schelling (1971) focused on a different – and in many ways more traditional – dimension of OC. For him, criminal groups engage primarily in various forms of extortion, and have exclusive (monopoly) control of a certain section of the (illicit) market; he thus refers to OC as "usually monopolized crime". Building on Cressey's earlier distinctions between ordinary and organised crime, Schelling notes that the latter tends to be more visible than the former, and should work to certain predictable and standardised rules if it is to be sustainable: the business has to be basically impersonal, and its "victims" have to be treated "fairly". Finally, the desire for monopoly helps to explain why there is often violent conflict between OC gangs – turf wars – but rarely between ordinary criminals.

In the 1980s, another leading criminologist, Alan Block (1980), described OC as part of a social system in which criminals, their clients and politicians were all involved in a reciprocal provision of services (see too Block and Chambliss 1981: esp. 63–114). This notion of collusion is a very important aspect of OC, and one to which we shall return at various points in this book. In the volume Block co-authored with William Chambliss (1981: 12), OC is defined as "a term that refers to those illegal activities connected with the management and coordination of racketeering (organized extortion) and the vices – particularly illegal drugs, illegal gambling, usury, and prostitution". Nowadays, such an approach looks a little dated and moralising; but it was an influential definition at the time.

Many academic analysts, as well as states (including the UK), see organised crime primarily as a form of illegal enterprise, in which criminal groups provide goods and services that are either illegal, in short supply, or considered over-priced in the legal market. Thus Phil Williams (2001: 106) writes that "Organized crime is perhaps best understood as the continuation of commerce by illegal means, with transnational criminal organizations as the illicit counterparts of multinational corporations." Others focus on different aspects of OC. Thus Peter Reuter (1994: esp. 94–6) sees the threat (endorsed by the group's reputation) or actual use of violence, plus durability, as the principal distinguishing features of criminal groups.

Howard Abadinsky has written what appears to be the most widely used English-language textbook on organised crime, which, as of early 2015, was in its tenth edition. He has modified his definition over the years, but now sees organised crime groups as having eight defining characteristics:

- They have no political goals (in earlier editions, this was couched in terms of them being non-ideological).
- They are hierarchically structured.
- They have limited or exclusive membership.
- They have a unique subculture (earlier versions of Abadinsky's list referred here to a division of labour rather than a subculture).
- They are self-perpetuating.
- They are willing to use illegal violence (in earlier editions, this variable also included reference to their willingness to use bribery).

- They are monopolistic – though less so transnationally than domestically/locally.
- They are governed by explicit rules and regulations (in earlier editions, there is a reference here to codes of honour).

Abadinsky goes on to argue that if a definition were to be limited to only two variables, they would be that OCGs are *non-ideological* and use *instrumental violence* (all from Abadinsky 2013: 2–5).

Some of these points are now dated, given significant changes that have occurred in the nature and style of criminal organisations in recent decades. For instance, while *some* gangs are still hierarchically structured and have strict rules on membership, others are much more fluid. Moreover, the increasing trend towards cybercrime in recent years means that OC now uses violence and even the threat of violence less than in the past.

In many ways, a more useful approach is that of James Finckenauer (2007: 5–9), who has proposed the following list of defining features:

- Lack of ideology;
- Structure/organised hierarchy (Finckenauer acknowledges that hierarchy is ever less of a distinguishing feature in contemporary organised crime, though it can still be found in, for instance, many biker – or outlaw motorcycle – gangs);
- Continuity;
- Violence/use of force or the threat of force;
- Restricted membership/bonding;
- Illegal enterprises (making profit, largely through the provision of goods and services that are illegal, regulated or in short supply; criminal organisations may also be involved in legal enterprise);
- Penetration of legitimate businesses; and
- Corruption (for example, of police, judiciary, politicians).

A much more general definition that can apply in all cases is Klaus von Lampe's (2001: 113 – adapting Becker 1966: 9) "organised crime is what people so label". While this has the attraction of being applicable in all cultures and contexts, it is too vague to operationalise. In other words, it would be difficult to conduct research into OC using such an approach.

Before moving to the next definitional aspect of OC, it is worth noting that Alan Wright (2006: 22–4) has argued that the term "transnational organised crime" reflects the politicisation of international law enforcement. For him and some other criminologists, the term "transnational" is often used by International Organisations (IOs) and powerful states such as the USA as a way of justifying interference in the law enforcement of smaller, less powerful countries. In short, Wright sees the term as politically loaded.

1.4   Disorganised crime

In a thought-provoking analysis, Rand Corporation economist Peter Reuter (1983) argued that the popular image of OC was largely misguided. Based on what he claimed to be more solid research than the FBI itself had conducted, and essentially in line with Block's (1980) empirically-based argument that much New York-based racketeering was very small-scale, Reuter maintained that most illegal gambling, illicit drug dealing and loan sharking, for instance, was run not by large hierarchical and enduring organisations such as the Mafia (usually referred to in the American context as La Cosa Nostra or LCN), but rather by a large number of small and often ephemeral enterprises, at least in the USA. He coined the term "disorganized crime" to describe this situation, and argued that the American LCN might in fact be a "paper tiger" – far less powerful and influential than the media and popular opinion maintained. In emphasising how small-scale much so-called organised (or what he preferred to call disorganised) crime was, Reuter was ahead of his time; as we have already seen, many of the current official definitions of OC indicate that a criminal group need comprise only three people to be classified as an example of OC.[2]

1.5   Organised crime and related concepts

How can OC be distinguished from other forms of crime, such as street crime or corporate crime? As Smith, Rush and Burton (2013) have pointed out, for example, the conceptual and practical distinctions between *street crime* and OC are often blurred. But one difference often highlighted is that the former is generally spontaneous, whereas the latter is by definition more structured and planned. As the name itself implies, street crime is also committed in public places, whereas much OC activity is committed clandestinely. Street crime is often random in selecting targets, and mostly affects ordinary members of the public, whereas OC tends to use violence or the threat of this against businesspeople or else targeted members of the public who fall behind in their payments for drugs, loans, and so on. Some have also observed that the average age of street gang members is generally lower than that of OCGs. Finally, and as already noted, Cressey sees OC as offering something to clients, usually goods or services, whereas many other forms of crime, including street crime, are purely predatory. Unfortunately, this particular distinction is potentially misleading, since many types of crime engaged in by OC do not offer anything to clients, but are purely predatory. The most we can say is that street crime is invariably predatory, whereas some forms of OC are not.

Turning to *corporate crime* – analysts such as Vincenzo Ruggiero (1996), Petrus van Duyne (2007) and to a limited extent Cressey (1972: 15–16) maintain that there is considerable overlap and similarity between the ways in which OC and many corporations operate. For instance, both criminal gangs and corporations have become increasingly transnational in recent decades, and both seek to maximise profits: many corporations try to do this by means that are either clearly illegal, or else in the grey area of legality but clearly unethical. An example of the latter is the measures adopted by many corporations to minimise their tax burdens by channelling profits through low-tax states rather than in the countries in which they were generated (the so-called Luxemburg scandal of late-2014 is a prime example – ICIJ 2014) or, particularly in the case of banks, to assist others to do this (for example, the HSBC scandal of 2015 – BBC 2015a). The similarities are such that these and other analysts question the use of the terms "underworld" and "upperworld" (the latter has been called the "overworld" by Schelling 1971: 644). Thus Cressey (1972: 14) writes:

> the "underworld" concept inaccurately suggests that the world's actors can readily be distinguished as either good guys ("upper") or bad guys ("under"). But in the United States, at least, the activities of many criminals are so closely linked with the activities of so-called "respectable" governmental officials and businessmen that it no longer makes sense to try to depict a separate "underworld" at all.

It will be obvious to most readers that this comment could be made about many countries today, not only the USA.

While there is much truth in the arguments just cited, there are also important differences between the ways in which corporations and crime gangs operate. Corporations are in general subject to much greater external scrutiny than OCGs are, and while the propensity of some gangs to seek to monopolise either a geographic region or a branch of crime (for example, drug trafficking) or both is similar to the drive of some corporations towards monopolisation, the latter are subject to anti-cartel laws in most countries. Corporations also have a legal responsibility to report their activities to the general public, the state, and, in particular, to their shareholders on a regular basis, whereas OCGs do not. And while corporations may seek to minimise their tax bills, criminal gangs typically pay no tax at all.

A final pair of terms to consider is *"mafia"* and organised crime. Many people, including most journalists, use these terms interchangeably. But a number of specialists draw a distinction between them. While seeing both as very similar and operating in many of the same ways and for the same reasons, the most important difference usually highlighted is that mafia-type organisations explicitly attempt to influence politics and interact with the political system, whereas other types of criminal organisation do not. However, some have drawn a second distinction. Thus Federico Varese (2001: 4–5), following Diego Gambetta (1993), sees a mafia group as a particular type of OCG – one that specialises in just one commodity, *viz.* protection.

1.6   Organised crime activities

OCGs engage in a wide variety of illegal activities, among the most common being (listed alphabetically rather than in order of significance, largely because the salience of each type varies so much from country to country and over time):

- ATM (a.k.a. a bancomat, a cashpoint or, in the UK, a hole in the wall) skimming – a card reader is surreptitiously and illegally attached to an automatic cash dispenser and captures the details of cards used in it, including pin codes; these details are then used by OC skimmers to withdraw funds from the victim's account or purchase goods.
- Blackmail – often of state officials or senior executives, so that a common response is for the blackmailed person to engage in corrupt acts that benefit the OCG that is threatening to reveal the person's misdemeanours.
- Contract killing – that is, murdering people on behalf of others who have paid (contracted) for this.

- Counterfeiting – for example of currencies, luxury items, DVDs, and so on.
- Cybercrime – computer-related crime, arguably the joint fastest growing organised crime activity; two common forms are online identity theft, and the often resultant identity fraud.[3]
- Document forgery – for example, of passports and visas.
- Fencing – wittingly purchasing stolen goods with the aim of selling them at a profit.
- Gambling – primarily in countries where this is illegal, though some groups also operate within legal gambling contexts.
- Kidnapping – forcibly seizing and hiding someone, and threatening to kill or harm them, usually unless a ransom is paid to have them released.
- Loan sharking – lending to people who find it difficult to secure a loan from a reputable source such as a bank, and at a much higher interest rate than could be obtained from such a source; this activity usually increases at times of serious economic problems, such as in the aftermath of the 2008 Global Financial Crisis (GFC).
- Match fixing – in sport, usually related to gambling.
- Money laundering – "cleaning" the improperly acquired funds of crime, nowadays usually by sending them abroad, depositing them in countries with opaque banking laws, and then withdrawing them and investing in legitimate projects (see Interpol 2015).
- Prostitution – primarily in countries where this is illegal, though some groups also operate within legalised sex work contexts.
- "Protection" – a potentially misleading term, since the so-called protection is mostly against the group selling it, though it can also be against rival OCGs or even law enforcement agencies.
- Smuggling – illegally moving humans, goods and services between countries. Some common forms are of:
  - antiquities
  - cigarettes
  - counterfeit goods (for example, CDs, DVDs and luxury leather goods)
  - endangered and rare flora and fauna
  - people
  - stolen vehicles.
- Theft – for example, of jewellery, money, identity.
- Trafficking – the illegal selling of humans, goods and services. While this is often linked to smuggling, it is conceptually

distinct (for a 7-point analysis of the differences between people smuggling and THB see Holmes 2014a: 25–6). Some common forms are of:

- animal products
- arms
- drugs
- endangered and rare species of animals and plants
- human organs
- humans (for forced labour, including sex work)
- manufactured products (for example, luxury goods).

This list is not exhaustive, but does provide a clear picture of just how broad the range of OC activities is.

1.7   Conclusions

By now, it will be obvious that there is considerable disagreement on the meaning and nature of OC. Some of these differences arise primarily from the fact that different analysts are focusing on different aspects of OC; whereas some emphasise violence or the threat thereof, others are primarily interested in OC as a particular type of business. Some – mostly older – approaches still refer to codes and hierarchical structures, whereas more recent ones stress the flexibility and loose structure of contemporary OC.

But while all definitions and taxonomies (in other words, listings of its various forms or types of activity; in addition to that cited above see Levi et al. 2013: 20) of this phenomenon are flawed and can be criticised, the seriousness of the problem requires us to use a problematic conceptual framework if we are to make any progress in containing it. The next chapter examines in detail this seriousness. Before proceeding to that, however, our own preferred approach needs to be specified. Rather than completely reinvent the wheel, we shall in this study opt basically for the current definition, cited above, of the UK's NCA; this allows for differing structures and group sizes, and does not refer to codes of honour or the role of OC in politics. In short, it allows for the considerable range of groups and activities that are nowadays labelled OC, and that is its strength. However, the NCA definition could at a push be used to define some forms of terrorism as well as OC. To overcome this, the phrase "Their motivation is often, but not always, financial gain" is replaced in our slightly modified version with the words

"Their primary motivation is usually financial gain." Furthermore, while acknowledging the validity of *some* of Wright's argument about the loaded nature of the concept of "transnational organised crime", the term is used here in the absence of anything better; after all, much OC activity *is* transnational.

NOTES

1 www.organized-crime.de/organizedcrimedefinitions.htm (accessed 23 November 2015).

2 The Scottish, Australian and Hong Kong governments, among others, require only *two* people to be classified as OC (Serious Organised Crime Taskforce 2009: 2; Australian Crime Commission 2007: 5; Hong Kong Government 2014 [latest version of 1994 legislation]: 2).

3 For the distinctions between these closely related concepts see www.freecreditscore.com/blog/identity-theft-identity-fraud/ (accessed 23 November 2015).

2   The impact of organised crime

While many of the potential effects of OC are obvious, others are less so. In this chapter, we begin by considering how individuals can be directly and indirectly affected by OC. We then examine the ways in which local communities, states and the international community are impacted. For the sake of a clearer exposition, these are considered in terms of the environmental, economic, social, cultural, political, security-related and international ramifications; in reality, the impact is often on two or more of these areas simultaneously.

2.1   Impact on individuals

It is clear from surveys that most ordinary citizens do not come into direct contact with OC. Yet the impact of OC is far more widespread than is often realised. We start by considering those aspects of which most people are aware, and then examine the less obvious ways in which OC affects almost all of us.

For many, the aspect of OC activity that first comes to mind is drug dealing. This is a major aspect of contemporary OC, and is commonly – and justifiably – associated with, for instance, biker gangs and Latin American drug cartels. At one stage, the US destruction of coca fields in Colombia and poppy fields in Afghanistan looked as if the so-called war on drugs might be having a real impact. But two developments mean that this was wishful thinking. The first is that coca growing (for cocaine) has simply moved elsewhere (for example, Bolivia, Chile and Peru) or gradually returned to various parts of Colombia, while Afghani opium growers have also made a comeback, and Myanmar (Burma) has long been an alternative source anyway. But another factor is the significant rise of synthetic drugs, such as crystalline methamphetamines (a.k.a. crank, crystal, ice and tina).

OC's supply of illicit drugs often has lethal effects on users. The most obvious one is that many addicts die of drug overdoses or from using impure drugs. But in addition, users who fall behind in their payments for these drugs can be subjected to violence, sometimes resulting in death.

It is not only illicit drugs that OC traffics. An increasing share of the illegal drug market is occupied by counterfeited versions of legal drugs that would normally be prescribed in more affluent societies by a doctor and obtained with a prescription; this is usually called pharmaceutical crime. In many parts of the world, access to a regular GP is difficult, because of distance, cost, and other factors. Under such circumstances, OCGs sometimes sell counterfeited painkillers, antibiotics, slimming pills, and so on. This can be highly profitable; one illegal online pharmaceutical network disbanded by US government authorities in 2011 had made approximately US$55 million over two years (Interpol 2014: 2).

Unfortunately, such counterfeit medicines are sometimes toxic because of the poor quality or incorrect proportions of – or simply the wrong – ingredients, resulting in sickness and sometimes death. In 2014, Interpol published a report on the involvement of OC in pharmaceutical crime since 2008 that suggested this had been increasing in many parts of the world, especially Latin America (Interpol 2014: 8). A major reason for this apparent increase is the rise of the Internet, which has made it easier for OCGs both to advertise their wares and evade law enforcement agencies, the latter because of the relative ease of ensuring anonymity on the Web. The Interpol report also noted that OC involvement in pharmaceutical crime is typically less structured than in more traditional types of OC activity, such as illicit drug trafficking and THB.

Another aspect of OC activity that often results in violence is illegal gambling. As with drug addicts who fall behind with their payments, many gamblers have been seriously beaten or have lost their lives at the hands of OC thugs for failing to pay back sums they have borrowed to feed their habit.

THB is a third area where OCGs frequently use violence, as well as deception. One typical situation relates to the earlier discussion of illicit drugs; human traffickers often force victims to take illicit drugs and become drug-dependent as a way of increasing control over them.

But there are many other ways in which OC uses violent means against THB victims. One is kidnapping. There are innumerable examples from around the world of gangs kidnapping people – especially women and children – so that they can be trafficked, often into prostitution; people who have not chosen to engage in sex work can be subject to both threatened and actual violence on a daily basis as they are coerced by their pimps into selling their bodies. This is a form of slavery, in which people are deprived of their most basic human rights (see Holmes 2010a).

An aspect of OC activity that affects a rapidly growing number of individuals is cybercrime. This assumes many forms, including phishing (online deception involving identity theft, often through the use of what look like official sites that encourage the user to reveal passwords, credit card details, and so on) and trojans (a.k.a. ransomware, in which criminals freeze a computer, claiming that a user has accessed illegal material such as child pornography, and demanding a ransom to free the computer). Many types of cybercrime are ultimately forms of fraud; as more and more of us make ever greater use of our computers, tablets and mobile phones to connect to the Internet, so an increasing percentage of the population will be victims of cybercrime (see Krebs 2014).

One form of OC activity that has grown in significance as we have become more dependent on technology is fraud based on ATM skimming. In Australia, there has been a marked increase in this form of fraud as gangs from Romania and Bulgaria, in particular, have used their new freedom to travel – both states joined the EU in 2007, which rendered it much easier to obtain visas to distant lands such as Australia – to visit other countries for a few weeks, skim a number of ATMs, and leave again much wealthier.

A less sophisticated form of fraud involves the theft of credit card details. In many countries, waiters can still take a credit card away – out of sight of its owner – to process it. During this time, criminals can either make a copy of the card, or merely jot down its details; in the latter case, they can then purchase goods online or by telephone from companies that have poor security. Unfortunately, many businesses deliberately have such inadequate security, since once they have the card details, the purchase is usually guaranteed; the suppliers have their money, and expect the banks to foot the bill.

Many analyses of the Sicilian Mafia have focused on its role in providing private protection in situations where, for various reasons, the state's protective agencies are ineffectual or unreliable. Thus Diego Gambetta (1993: 1) defines the Mafia as "a specific economic enterprise, an industry which produces, promotes and sells private protection". While the Mafia and other OCGs do sometimes provide protection to parties engaged in illicit transactions, as well as against business competitors, they also often "offer" protection against the gang itself or other OC syndicates. In many parts of the world, such "protection" is in essence forced on citizens running small enterprises such as shops, restaurants, bars, taxi companies, and so on. While such OC activity is (justifiably) often associated with Italian OC or LCN (the US Mafia), an experiment conducted by the BBC's *Panorama* team in Liverpool in 2007–8 revealed that protection racketeering was a significant problem in the Merseyside area too (BBC One 2008).

Finally, OC can blackmail businesspeople, politicians and others. For instance, a politician might be desperate to hide something from the public (for example, a drug habit) or from his/her family (for example, an illicit love affair), and pays an OCG to have this kept secret.

2.2   Impact on societies, states and the international community

2.2.1   Environmental effects

Many consider the environment to be the single biggest issue humanity needs to address in the twenty-first century. Unfortunately, OC has become increasingly involved in illegal activities that seriously harm the environment. In a recent UNODC publication (Lale-Demoz and Lewis 2013) that focuses on TOC in the Asia-Pacific region, three chapters are devoted to the role of TOC in activities that are seriously detrimental to the environment, and thus ultimately to us all – illegal wildlife trade; illicit trade in wood-based products; and illicit trade in electrical and electronic waste. Each of these can be briefly considered.

Many species of animal – fauna – are either on an endangered list or already near extinction. Yet, while many governments and international agencies seek to protect such species, OC seeks to profit from their rarity, with no care that they might soon be extinct (Wyatt 2013). A prime motivator for OC gangs is the huge profits they can make from selling illegal animal products for traditional Asian medicines and other purposes. These include ivory (from elephant tusks, for carved ornaments); tiger bone (for virility); and rhinoceros horn (for fever, rheumatism, and dagger handles in Yemen – on all this see Davies 2005; Rademeyer 2012; Lale-Demoz and Lewis 2013: 75–86; Orenstein 2013). Some idea of the scale such criminality can assume is provided by the data generated by a May 2015 coordinated operation mounted across three continents (Africa, Asia and Europe) by law enforcement agencies from 62 countries working with Interpol and Europol. This operation – "Cobra III" – resulted in over 300 arrests, and more than 600 seizures of animal products, including over twelve tons of elephant tusks, 126 rhinoceros horns, and 16 whale ribs (Guardian 2015).

Animals are not the only form of living thing – in addition to humans and human organs (on the latter see Meyer 2006; Territo and Matteson 2012) – trafficked by OCGs. Rare plants and seeds (flora) can also be profitable. But a more common product is timber and wooden products. Countries in which "timber mafias" play a significant role include Brazil, Democratic Republic of the Congo, India, Indonesia and Russia. According to a UN report (Nellemann and Interpol 2012: 13 – citing a 2009 Interpol and World Bank report), 50–90 per cent of timber harvested in tropical countries and 15–30 per cent of global forest production is logged illegally. When it is borne in mind that an estimated 17 per cent of all emissions produced by human activity is the result of deforestation, and that this represents some 50 per cent more than the amount of pollution produced by all forms of transport combined (aviation, land transport and shipping), the impact of OC on global warming comes sharply into focus.

Disposal of electronic waste is another area in which OC has become very active. This growth has been a function of our increasing use and ever more frequent replacement of electronic products, notably computers and mobile phones. Such items can be properly recycled, but it is often quicker, simpler and cheaper to recycle illegally, without the safety controls involved in legitimate recycling. Among the numerous problems arising from this branch of OC activity is that various toxins are produced and allowed to float off into the atmosphere, with potentially serious consequences for health.

Finally, OC groups have been accused of trafficking nuclear waste. A prime example is the Italian OC syndicate 'Ndrangheta, which has been accused of trafficking waste to Somalia in the 1980s and 1990s in return for payment from European and American firms and organisations that found it difficult to dispose of such waste via legal means (Bocca 2005; Kington 2007; Woodfall 2007).

2.2.2   Economic effects

As with many aspects of OC activity, most people are unaware of the extent to which they are affected by economic crimes committed by OC. The impact of economic cybercrime and ATM-skimming on individuals has already been mentioned, so that the focus is now on the less obvious ways in which economies are affected by OC activity.

Actual estimates of the impact of OC on economies are considered in the next chapter. Here, it can be noted that since most OC activity is by definition illegal, criminal organisations do not generally declare their income to the authorities, which in turn means that states' tax revenues are lower than they should be; the more OC there is in a given jurisdiction, the worse this problem. This has knock-on effects for the general public, since reduced revenue means fewer and poorer services are provided by the state. Ironically, this often includes policing, so that a vicious circle is created; fewer law enforcement resources make it easier for OC to operate, and thus further to reduce state revenue.

States incur additional costs because of OC. For example, it has been estimated that the combined economic and social costs arising from illicit Class A (the most harmful – including heroin, cocaine, LSD and ecstasy) drug abuse in England and Wales alone in 2003–4 was more than £15 billion. While it might be expected that the principal economic cost relating to illicit drug use is healthcare, this accounts for only some 9 per cent of total costs. The lion's share of these costs – almost 90 per cent – relates to crimes such as burglary and theft that are committed by people under the influence of illicit drugs (all data from Dubourg and Prichard 2007: 23, 27–8).

The establishment of the Financial Action Task Force (FATF, see Chapter 7) in 1989 was primarily a reaction to the rapidly growing scale of money laundering. This phenomenon has been growing in recent decades. Like so many aspects of OC activity, its clandestine nature means that we cannot produce accurate statistics on its scale. However, in a report produced by the UNODC (2011a: 7), it was estimated, using the best available methodologies, that all OC activity combined (domestic and transnational) accounted for 3.6 per cent of global GDP in 2009, with at least 2.7 per cent being laundered. These percentages might appear small until it is realised that the sum being laundered was equivalent to some US$1.6 *trillion*, or the total output of the Spanish economy (FATF 2015).

OC seeks to launder its ill-gotten gains in various ways. FATF (2015) has described the three stages through which money laundering typically progresses. The first involves breaking up large sums into much smaller ones and depositing these in a number of banks; since an increasing number of countries require banks to report large deposits that can then be investigated by state authorities, it would be foolish of a criminal organisation to place large amounts in just one or two banks. The second stage is "layering", which typically involves attempts to move the funds offshore. A common method is to establish shell companies, that is, "companies" that are empty "shells", in that they do not in fact produce anything or provide any services, but to which illicit funds can be transferred. The third and final stage is "integration", which basically means releasing these funds into the legitimate economy. Thus the funds might be used to purchase shares, invest in legal businesses, or to purchase expensive durable goods, including real estate.

The focus so far in this subsection has been mainly on ways in which OC can cheat the state of revenue and increase costs to the state and society. But OC activity often also has a significant direct impact on legitimate businesses. If OC is able to avoid paying taxes and employer costs (for example, superannuation contributions for employees), it can provide unfair competition to legitimate businesses that are paying these overheads. Although much OC activity involves the provision of goods and services not usually supplied by legitimate businesses – which therefore does not compete with these businesses – some also involves what are on one level legitimate goods and services. For instance, OC might sell everyday goods in a local market that have been either stolen or else produced by trafficked labour; shoppers looking for a bargain will buy these goods rather than the same products at a higher price in a legitimate sales outlet.

Cybercrime is having a growing impact on economies around the world. According to one estimate, the annual cost of cybercrime globally is now in excess of $400 billion, and may be much higher (CSIS 2014: 2, 4–6). A closely related and growing problem, primarily for developed states, is the theft of intellectual property (IP). While this is sometimes undertaken by states – China has frequently been accused of this – OC is also often deeply involved. This has traditionally been in counterfeit products such as DVDs that are sold in markets and even well-known stores. But as OC has become more sophisticated, some groups now engage in complex forms of industrial espionage, selling their findings to both legitimate private firms and some states. This has negative economic implications for the companies and research institutions from which the IP has been stolen. The USA's National Crime Prevention Council (NCPC) has identified one of the most violent Mexican OC gangs – Los Zetas – as being heavily involved in IP theft from US companies (NCPC 2015).

2.2.3   Social effects

There are numerous – if sometimes less than obvious – ways in which OC impacts negatively on society. One is on crime rates. According to official statistics, almost 20 per cent of prisoners in the US in 2004 claimed that they had committed their crimes to obtain funds for the purchase of drugs (Dorsey and Middleton n.d.: 1), while a January 1998 US report claimed that some 80 per cent of US inmates had been under the influence of either illicit drugs or alcohol at the time they committed their crimes (Wren 1998). In a nuanced and sophisticated analysis of the costs of drug-related crime in the UK, the authors argue that:

> The cost imposed on society by heroin users' drug-induced crime is extremely high if we include an allowance for the distress as well as tangible losses experienced by victims and for the costs of reactive policing and criminal justice procedures. (Bryan, Del Bono and Pudney 2013: 27)

While numerous methodological problems mean we cannot provide definitive data on the impact of illicit drug use on crime rates, there is no question that the effect is significant, and that OC plays a major role in this.

It was noted above that cybercrime is having an effect on an increasing number of citizens around the world, as more and more people have their accounts hacked and personal data stolen. When it is borne in mind that Bill Gates, Bill Clinton, Interpol and the Pentagon have all been hacked – albeit not in all cases by OC – it becomes clear that no-one who goes online can be certain that they are secure against this form of criminal activity. In addition to the growing sense of uncertainty among individuals about using the Web for online banking, purchasing goods and services, applying for visas, and so on, this type of crime can impact negatively on legitimate employment in developed countries. Thus it is argued in a report by the Washington-based Center for Strategic and International Studies (CSIS 2014: 3) that one of the effects of OC is "to shift employment away from jobs that create the most value"; it estimates that up to 200,000 American jobs and 150,000 EU positions could be lost as a result of cybercrime. If cybercriminals steal know-how from country A in the developed world and either sell that to other countries (B) or themselves set up factories or workshops – quite possibly using trafficked labour – then jobs in those sectors are lost in country A. The CSIS (2014: 13) report cites a European company that had to cut its workforce in half after some of its IP was stolen by hackers; through the latters' activity, another firm was able essentially to duplicate the European company's product and compete with it. Cybercrime can also increase social problems relating to online gambling addiction, with all the costs to society relating to this.

Together with cybercrime, THB is believed to be the fastest growing form of OC activity. This clearly has a serious negative impact on those trafficked, who become essentially slaves. But THB also has negative effects on society more generally. For instance, higher numbers of trafficked sex workers are likely to increase the prevalence of sexually transmitted diseases, including HIV/AIDS. An influx of trafficked labourers can increase unemployment rates among the local population of legal workers. This in turn can increase social tensions, including racism if the trafficked labourers are predominantly foreigners.

Before moving to the next section, it is important to note that OC can have even less tangible but nevertheless significant effects on a society, such as undermining its moral fabric. Another is that OC can lead to reduced levels of trust in a society, and therefore of positive social capital – while at the same time promoting negative social capital, such as the attractiveness to some of a criminal lifestyle and membership of a gang.

2.2.4   Cultural effects

Culture – here referring primarily to what Raymond Williams (1976: 80) has defined as "the works and practices of intellectual and especially artistic activity" – is not something most people would associate with (T)OC. But in recent times, OC has come to realise that one of the best ways to launder its ill-gotten gains is to purchase artwork. As De

Sanctis (2013) argues, while art can be a solid investment anyway, the "discreet" emphasis many art dealers place on the anonymity of their clients, and the significant value of high end art works (that is, so that a large sum of money can be paid – laundered – for a single painting or sculpture, for example) makes investment in such creative products attractive to a growing number of criminals.

The enormous sums collectors will pay for cultural artefacts have also been noticed by OC gangs, who steal and then traffic such items. Doing so often deprives the general public of part of their own heritage and culture (on Chinese OC doing this, and for an explanation of how, see Lo 2008: 23–4).

2.2.5   Political effects

As noted in Chapter 1, some analysts distinguish mafias from other forms of OC primarily in that the former directly and consciously interact with political elites, whereas the latter seek to steer clear of the state. Thus the Sicilian Mafia has in the past been closely related to the Christian Democracy party that governed Italy from just after the Second World War to 1994. OC has played a role in limiting electoral competition in many countries, which undermines the democratic process. In Japan, the Yakuza have often been directly involved with major political parties. For instance, in 2007, Japan's largest OCG, the Kobe-based Yamaguchi-gumi, decided to support the Democratic Party of Japan (DPJ), allegedly in return for a promise from a senior DPJ politician that if the party won the upcoming election, it would delay indefinitely a proposed criminal conspiracy law (Adelstein 2010, 2012). In some countries, Russia being a good example, individuals under suspicion of or actual investigation for OC activity have contested elections and avoided further investigation by having themselves elected, thereby enjoying parliamentary immunity.

At the beginning of the millennium, the World Bank published analyses of what it called "state capture" (see Hellman et al. 2000). Initially, this focused on the ways in which usually licit companies seek in a non-transparent manner to bribe the state's legislators to adopt decisions beneficial to those businesses. But as the debate on state capture has developed, it has become clear that OC can also seek to influence legislators through illicit and often illegal means. Unfortunately, surveys reveal that many citizens in democratic systems do not wish to fund political parties. Yet democracy is not a cost-free good, and as campaigning becomes more expensive while legitimate sources of party financing become more difficult to secure, so the more vulnerable politics becomes to the temptations offered by OC.

In the early-1990s, a new term – "parapolitics" – emerged in social science to describe what Robert Cribb (2009: 1) has called "a strange, powerful, clandestine and apparently structural relationship between state security-intelligence apparatuses, terrorist organisations and transnational organised criminal syndicates". It will be demonstrated in Chapter 4 that a major source of recruits for OC in many states is the security services; this is highly compatible with Cribb's point. There is mounting evidence from many countries of collusion between state officials on the one hand – notably police officers, customs officers, and politicians – and OC on the other. Thus Cribb's chapter appears in a collection (Wilson and Lindsey 2009) that provides case studies of the collusion between (T)OC and governments in Afghanistan, Colombia, Italy, Mexico and the Philippines; since several of these countries also have a reputation for high levels of OC activity and violence, the implications of such collusion are all too obvious (for recent examples of alleged police collusion with OC see Wilson 2014; Gecker 2015).

One final possibility is for OC to challenge the political system directly, as a way of undermining it and demonstrating OC's greater power. A prime example is furnished by the actions of Brazilian drug syndicates starting in September 2002, when the "Comando Vermelho" – one of Rio de Janeiro's most powerful drug trafficking gangs – shut down public transport, schools and shops to show local authorities that they (the drug syndicate) were more powerful than the state; this practice has been repeated since (Penglase 2005).

But these overt ways in which OC can have detrimental effects on political systems are not the only ones. At a deeper and more abstract level, OC's involvement with politics can undermine a regime's – and possibly even a system's – legitimacy; if citizens believe that state officials routinely liaise with OCGs, they will not trust and therefore will not normatively support the state.

2.2.6   Security and international effects

There is by now ample proof of the significant role OC can and often does play in undermining the security of states and societies; the delegitimation role just described is only one of them. In addition to the impact of OC on state revenue that affects how much is available for law enforcement and that has already been noted, OC plays a significant role in arms smuggling and trafficking. There is evidence – some of it hard, some of it strongly circumstantial – that OCGs have either sold weapons to, or traded weapons for drugs with, terrorist and paramilitary organisations. Examples include deals between Russian OC and both Russian and Afghan terror groups, notably the Taliban (Curtis 2002; see too UNAMA 2015); various OC groups and terrorists in the Tri-Border area of Paraguay, Brazil and Argentina (Shelley and Picarelli 2005: 60–5); and FARC (Revolutionary Armed Forces of Colombia) and the Mexico-based Arellano Felix Organisation (Miró, 2003: 7; for further examples and analysis see Kartha 2000; Curtis and Karacan 2002; Hutchinson and O'Malley 2007; Schori Liang 2011).

Moreover, a number of terrorist organisations are themselves now engaging in OC to fund their activities (Hill 2005: 47; Hough 2011). The USA's National Security Council (2011) reported that several of the 63 groupings on the Department of Justice's 2010 "Consolidated Priority Organization Targets" list of organisations threatening the USA were terrorist groups that were now involved in drug trafficking; among these were the Taliban, FARC, Hezbollah and possibly al-Qaeda.

Ironically, the tendency for terrorist groups to engage in OC activity themselves, as distinct from collaborating and trading with existing OCGs, appears to have increased as a direct result of the West's reaction to the 9/11 terrorist attack on the USA. Thus Thomas Sanderson (2004) argues that the measures adopted by states and IOs to clamp down on financial flows to terrorist organisations have led some of the latter to engage in traditional OC activities, including money laundering and drug trafficking. Conversely, the UNODC (2010: 229–31) has demonstrated that reducing the production and trafficking of illicit drugs correlates with a decline in terrorist activity, at least in Latin America. One other point to note is that whereas "trade" between OCGs and terrorist organisations is generally cooperative, the relationship becomes competitive – sometimes violently so – when the latter decide to engage in OC activity, such as drug trafficking, themselves (Martin 2014: 164).

One of the few positive aspects of the increasing security risk of (T)OC and the convergence or transformation of terrorism with/into OC is that it has encouraged much greater cooperation between law enforcement agencies across many jurisdictions, as well as more determined moves to agree on common definitions of OC and methods for measuring it (see Chapter 3).

2.3   Conclusions

The focus in this chapter has been overwhelmingly on the *negative* effects of OC on states, societies, and the international community. But it is sometimes argued that there are situations in which OC can play a positive role. For instance, Japanese Yakuza groups have on occasion assisted ordinary citizens in the aftermath of natural disasters, such as earthquakes; a prime example is the aid they provided immediately following the major March 2011 earthquake and tsunami in Japan. Many historians of the Sicilian Mafia (for example, Hess 1998: 15–38) argue that the organisation arose largely because local government was so ineffective; the Mafia played some of the roles that would normally be expected of states or local authorities. And some maintain that people smugglers can play a positive role in helping people from underprivileged and post-conflict situations to counter the exclusionary policies of many developed states, thus increasing their human rights; surveys indicate that many citizens of Fujian Province in China are of this view, for example.

While there is some validity to these arguments, it needs to be borne in mind that the occasional positives are always outweighed by stronger negatives sooner or later. Thus the type of protection the Yakuza and the Mafia have offered over decades often involves threats of or actual violence. The ability of the Yakuza to assist in the aftermath of natural disasters is dependent on their capacity to acquire funds through illegal methods. Furthermore, when it is borne in mind that people smuggling all too often mutates into THB, and that even smuggled people who do not become trafficking victims are in most cases unable to enjoy the welfare benefits or freedom to travel enjoyed by citizens of their destination country, it becomes clear that the alleged positives in terms of human rights need to be analysed soberly in light of reality.

A final point that has been touched upon in this chapter, but is so important that it needs to be reiterated here, is that (T)OC could not have nearly as much impact as it does were it not for collusion by corrupt officials of the state. This sometimes occurs in the form of "turning a blind eye" in return for bribes (money, consumer durables, sex, and so on), sometimes through warning OCGs of imminent raids or stakeouts, and sometimes through direct involvement with gangs in various forms of OC activity, such as THB, drug trafficking, oil smuggling to and from countries subject to sanctions, and the illegal acquisition of weapons.[1] While OC can be criticised for corrupting officials, the latter must be castigated for accepting favours from gangs.

NOTE

1 On the connections with THB see PACO 2002; UNODC 2011b. Note also that the OECD has now
   – as of 2015 – explicitly focused on the often close connections between corruption and THB, and
   is currently working on guidelines to address the problem.

3   Measuring organised crime

Measuring the scale of OC is highly problematic. We have already seen (Chapter 1) that neither organisations nor academic specialists can fully agree on what constitutes OC, which is one obvious reason why measurement is so difficult; many other reasons will emerge below. But despite the numerous problems involved, it is necessary to form some impression of the nature and scale of OC if we are to maximise the effectiveness of attempts to combat it.

In this chapter, we consider three main approaches to the measurement of OC, each of which subdivides into two or more subsections: the three are official statistics; business perception and experience surveys; and alternative methods. An introductory caveat is that there is an overemphasis here on European and post-communist states. This is partly because of the author's own primary area of research, but more because of two further factors. One is that some of the most detailed survey information available has only been gathered in such countries. The other is that the "alternative methods" have mainly been devised and deployed in Europe.

3.1   Official statistics

There are two main types of official statistics (that is, those produced by governments and IOs) on OC, legal and economic. The first of these can typically be subdivided into five types:

- Reports – how many allegations of OC activity have been reported to the law enforcement authorities in a given period (usually one year)?
- Investigations – how many investigations of alleged (reported by the public or the media), suspected (law enforcement agencies have their own reasons for believing criminal activity is occurring or has occurred), and actual (in other words, there is no doubt that

a crime has been committed by a group, but evidence needs to be gathered) cases of OC have been mounted during a given period?

- Prosecutions – how many investigations have resulted in members of a group being sent to court to answer charges (the indictment)? In countries that produce detailed legal statistics, both the number of cases and the number of individuals charged will be given.
- Convictions – how many prosecutions result in people being found guilty and penalised?
- Sentences meted out (fines; suspended and actual prison sentences; death sentences; etc.). An important question to consider here is whether the penalties in one jurisdiction typically appear much more lenient (or harsher) for a similar type of crime than those meted out in another jurisdiction.

At first sight, official statistics might appear to be a reliable source of information on the scale and nature of OC. However, they must be treated with caution, and usually as *minimum* indications of the scale. Unfortunately, even this is not a watertight assumption, since OC activity will sometimes be included in the total number of a particular type of crime, such as fraud or car theft, that has been committed by both OCGs and individuals. In this case, the number of OC cases will be less than the total number of fraud or car theft cases reported; but unless a disaggregated figure on the actual number of such cases committed by OCGs is reported, which is rare, all we know is that the official statistic on that particular type of crime is almost certainly *higher* than the number of cases involving OC. We can now consider each of the five types of statistic in turn and see why each may raise further problems.

In the case of reports, it needs to be noted who is reporting and why. In many cases, the people reporting are unreliable. Thus a criminal might be an informant, reporting on – and either exaggerating or even completely fabricating – the activities of other criminals so as to gain favour with the law enforcement agencies (for example, to reduce or avoid a penalty, so-called plea bargaining), or as a way of seeking revenge on fellow-criminals who have betrayed the reporting criminal. There are also serial reporters – people who, for reasons that include mental illness or loneliness, frequently contact the law enforcement agencies with spurious information. It can be challenging and time-consuming for the police to separate the wheat (genuine and reliable reports) from the chaff (mischievous or misguided reports).

The number of investigations can relate to the reporting cultures and structural aspects of a given law enforcement agency. For instance, in countries where crime detection targets are set, the agency might be penalised for not investigating enough reports – or rewarded for exceeding targets. This point about culture and structural (or systemic) conditions also applies to the number of prosecutions and convictions, as well as to the type and number of sentences meted out. Thus governments might be under pressure from either the public or IOs to "do something" about OC, and so pressure the judiciary to maximise the number of sentences and apply as severe penalties as the law permits.

In addition to legal statistics, governments, IOs and NGOs also sometimes produce data on various aspects of the economic impact or scale of OC. The methodologies used to produce such measurements are often very technical, and beyond the scope of an introductory text. But it should be obvious that the clandestine nature of much OC activity means that, however sophisticated our measurement methods become, a certain amount of subjectivity and guesswork will always be involved.

Bearing this important point in mind, let us consider some of the most well-regarded assessments. According to one official estimate, TOC globally generated US$870 *billion*, or 1.5 per cent of the world's total GDP, in 2009 (UNODC 2011a: 7). A 2013 report from the European Parliament (Levi et al. 2013: 10–11) estimated that the *minimum* direct economic cost of OC to the EU was almost 170 billion euros. In the UK alone, according to an estimate commissioned by the Home Office (Dubourg and Prichard 2006: iii), the economic and social costs of OC amounted to £24.5 billion in the early-2000s.

While all statistics estimating the economic costs of OC's activities have to be treated with caution, some figures cited in the public domain raise serious doubts. For example, a leading Russian newspaper with traditionally close ties to the government, *Izvestiya*, claimed in January 1994 that Russian OC controlled some 70–80 per cent of banking and private business in the country; this figure is so high that it must be treated with scepticism. The world's leading NGO for addressing corruption, Transparency International, claimed in a 2007 report that for every 100 officially recorded euros of capital in Albania, there are 80 euros of unrecorded, most of which are the proceeds of OC. Even more incredible is that Albanian analyses between 2003 and 2007 suggested that for every one euro legally invested, five were illegally invested (Michaletos and Markos 2007). Again, such figures are such that one must keep an open mind as to their reliability. Since official statistics are so problematic, let us now consider alternative ways of measuring the scale and impact of OC.

3.2   Business perception and experience surveys

One of the most useful guides to the scale of OC activity is perceptions surveys. In one of the best known of these, the World Economic Forum's *Global Competitiveness Report* (GCR), respondents are asked about their views on the extent to which they believe their business is affected by OC. Table 3.1 provides responses to this question from various countries. The criteria for inclusion in this table are threefold:

1.   Countries that are the home base for major TOC groupings examined in detail in Chapter 4.
2.   Major Anglophone countries (given the dominant readership of this book).
3.   Countries not included in categories 1 or 2 and considered to be major centres of THB.

One disturbing point to emerge from Table 3.1 is that OC is perceived by businesspeople to be a problem even in countries not usually considered to have much of a problem with it, such as Australia and the UK. Another is that OC was perceived to be a *worse* problem in 2014 than in 2010 in every country apart from Bulgaria, where the improvement was extremely marginal anyway; the deterioration was particularly marked in several Central and East European (CEE) states (Albania, Moldova, and especially Romania).

Some critics of perception surveys argue that they do not reflect reality. This is an unconvincing criticism, for two reasons. First, perceptions are a form of reality; businesses, for instance, make important decisions on the basis of perceptions about future market conditions. Second, there is often an implicit assumption in this criticism that someone knows the "real" scale of OC activity; this is simply untrue, so that it is actually the critics who are being unrealistic. Nevertheless, criticism of perception surveys has contributed to the development of experience-based surveys; sometimes, experiential questions are included with perceptual ones in questionnaires.

Table 3.1   Question: to what extent does organised crime (mafia-oriented racketeering, extortion) impose costs on businesses in your country? [1 = significant costs; 7 = no costs]

	2010 (Score)	2010 (Global rank)	2014 (Score)	2014 (Global Rank)
Albania	5.2	82	4.3	95
Australia	6.2	32	5.9	23
Bulgaria	3.9	124	4.0	117
Cambodia	4.9	90	4.5	86
Canada	5.8	50	5.3	50
China	5.2	76	4.7	70
Italy	3.7	130	3.3	132
Japan	5.3	71	5.2	52
Mexico	2.9	136	2.7	140
Moldova	5.3	68	4.6	83
Nigeria	4.2	119	3.7	124
Romania	5.9	43	4.1	105
Russia	4.3	112	4.2	101
Serbia	4.3	111	4.1	106
Thailand	5.1	83	4.5	89
United Kingdom	6.0	39	5.8	29
United States	5.1	86	4.7	73

Notes: The scores are given to only one decimal place, but were originally computed to a more precise level; this explains how two countries – for example, Thailand and the USA in 2010 – can have the "same" score but be differently ranked.
2010 – N = 139; 2014 – N = 144

Sources: 2010 – Schwab 2010: 380; 2014 – Schwab 2014: 420.

One of the best known of such experiential surveys is the *Business Environment and Economic Performance Survey* (BEEPS) produced jointly by the European Bank for Reconstruction and Development and the World Bank. Unfortunately, although this has been conducted on several occasions since the first survey in 1999, only once – in 2005 (EBRD–World Bank 2005) – was a question asked directly about business' actual experience of OC activity; in other years, the question refers to crime generally, and is therefore of no use to us. However, a report by the European Bank for Reconstruction and Development indicated that, while still a bigger problem for post-communist transition states than the aggregate score for three "mature market economies" (Germany, Greece and Portugal), OC had declined in significance for the former between 1999 and 2005 (EBRD 2005: 69). If this finding and the earlier ones cited from the GCR reflect reality, the picture is depressing; in contrast to the improvements in the early-2000s, the situation appears to have been deteriorating lately.

A more recent survey of businesses that included questions on their experiences of OC was "The Crime against Businesses in Europe" report commissioned by the EU and conducted across 20 EU member-states in 2012. At first glance, these results were encouraging; while theft by unknown persons and burglary had been experienced by some 11–12 per cent of businesses in the previous twelve months, "the lowest prevalent rate values were registered for protection money (0.4%), extortion (0.6%), bribery and corruption (1.0%) and usury (1.0%)"; since these are crimes typically associated with OC (usury being loan sharking), they may provide some indication of the scale of OC activity in EU member states. However, the authors of the report point out that businesses were less likely to report their experiences of these crimes honestly than they were of crimes such as burglary and vandalism, "since they imply an active involvement of the businesses or the interviewees in an illicit or irregular activity". Surprisingly, the EU member state whose businesses reported the most experience of having to pay protection money was Slovenia (all from Dugato et al. 2013: 22–3; 52–3).

Another pair of surveys that can help us to create a patchwork picture of the OC situation around the world is the ICCS (International Commercial Crime Survey) and the ICBS (International Crime Business Survey). Unfortunately, these have only been conducted twice, in 1994 and 2000 respectively, and only in a limited number of countries (nine in 1994 – Australia, Czechia, France, Germany, Hungary, Italy, the Netherlands, Switzerland and the United Kingdom – with limited data from a tenth country, South Africa; and only in the *capitals* of nine post-communist states in 2000 – Albania, Belarus, Bulgaria, Croatia, Hungary, Lithuania, Romania, Russia and Ukraine), and mostly in smaller enterprises. Nevertheless, given the paucity of survey data, it is worth highlighting some of the surveys' principal findings.

The 1994 survey was conducted primarily among retail businesses. Frustratingly, the results were not directly comparable across all the countries, and in any case focused on corruption, fraud and general crime (for example, burglary and theft, shoplifting, vandalism).

However, some parts of the questionnaires did implicitly relate to OC. Thus respondents were asked if crimes such as "extortion by government officials or others, demands for 'protection money', blackmailing" and similar criminal activities occurred in their sector. Perhaps surprisingly, 16 per cent of respondents interviewed in the Netherlands claimed that such practices occurred "often" or "rather often", while this figure reached a high 45 per cent among entrepreneurs in the catering industry (van Dijk and Terlouw 1996: 160–1).

The sample sizes in the CEE capitals in 2000 ranged from 316 in Minsk (Belarus) to 532 in Sofia (Bulgaria), and the responses make for interesting reading. While corruption was seen as even more of a problem than "crime and insecurity" across the CEE region, one set of questions related explicitly to "intimidation and extortion", and was thus of direct relevance to our focus on OC. On average, 9 per cent of businesses had experienced intimidation and extortion during 1999, a figure that rose to a very high 29 per cent of businesses victimised in this way in Minsk. In the Belarusian capital, moreover, some 33 per cent of businesses had received requests in the previous year for protection money; the average across the nine capitals was much lower – but still disturbingly high – at 8 per cent. Another point of real concern was that, of those subject to OC intimidation, approximately 9 per cent involved a direct threat of violence with weapons. Finally, and yet another cause for concern, some 70 per cent of respondents across the region did not report OC threats and actions to the police, primarily because of a lack of confidence in the law enforcement agencies: this in turn was above all a function of the perceived corruption levels among police officers (all from Alvazzi del Frate 2004: 150–2, 157). This is clear evidence of the perceived high level of collusion between the police and OC in many countries.

Most of the other comparative surveys on crime, such as the International Crime Victim Survey (ICVS), relate to crime generally rather than OC specifically, and thus are of no direct relevance here. We can speculate that one of the reasons for this is that ordinary citizens either do not wittingly come into direct contact with OC (unlike businesses, which are often subject to protection rackets), or else do not wish to report this, since they fear losing access to a product, such as illicit drugs, for which they are dependent on OC.

3.3   Alternative methods

3.3.1   COCI

While perceptual and experiential surveys remain one of the most useful methods for attempting to discover the scale and nature of OC activity, there has been a move in recent years, particularly among West European specialists, to develop alternative measurement tools. One of the most innovative if controversial is the Composite Organised Crime Index (COCI) devised by Dutch criminologist Jan van Dijk. Employing data from a number of different sources (official crime statistics; the World Economic Forum; Merchant International Group's assessments of investment risks in 150 countries; and studies by the World Bank Institute) primarily for the years 1996–2004, van Dijk estimates the scale and significance of OC around the world on the basis of five variables:

- The perceived prevalence of OC.
- Unsolved murders (van Dijk argues that most murders are either crimes of passion, which are usually solved, or gangland murders, which are not, and cites Latin American "proof" to support his case).
- The level of grand (elite) corruption.
- The scale of money laundering.
- The extent of the black economy.

He produces a score for each variable, and then an aggregate score for sixteen regions of the world. Using this method, the three regions least affected by OC appear to be Oceania, West and Central Europe, and North America, whereas those most impacted are Eastern Europe, Central Asia and Transcaucasia, and the Caribbean (van Dijk 2007: 42, 2008: 163). Based on his findings, van Dijk (2007: 43) argues that "Within Europe, organized crime prevalence increases diagonally from the north west to the south east, with levels being low in England and Germany, higher in Spain and Italy and by far the highest in Russia, Albania and Ukraine." However, the fact that four of the five variables are based on soft data means that these conclusions must be treated warily.

3.3.2   Threat (risk) assessments

An increasing number of criminologists and police forces have in recent years been adopting threat (or risk – sometimes a.k.a. vulnerability) assessments in their attempts to identify where OC is most likely to constitute a serious problem. One of the first police forces to have used this is the German Federal Criminal Office, which has since 1999 been including an "organised crime potential" of particular groups in its annual (since 1992) report on OC. According to von Lampe's (2005: 230) analysis of this approach, three questions need to be addressed in assessing this potential:

- What, basically, is OC?
- What are OC's crucial properties in terms of impact and social consequences?
- How can valid and reliable data be obtained?

One final but important point to note from von Lampe's analysis is his emphasis on the need to consider the market context when assessing OC threats: changing demand for illegal products and services, for instance, will normally mean that OC gangs will shift their attention to potentially more lucrative, higher demand products and services.

This point about researching the market is also strongly emphasised in an analysis of the qualitative risk- or threat-based methodology used by the Belgian police since 2001. Tom Vander Beken maintains that a modern approach to assessing the threat from OC should not involve analysis of specific groups and their salient characteristics; analyses should be structural rather than personalised, and focus on changing market demand and context. His proposed method comprises three parts – "environmental scanning, analysis of organizations and counter strategies and licit and illicit sector analysis" (Vander Beken 2004: 471 and *passim*); by environment, he is referring to the context and climate in which OC is operating.

Vander Beken further maintains that OC itself has to conduct risk assessment and be adaptable. One way in which it can reduce risk is to interact increasingly with legitimate commercial organisations. But when such methods fail or are inadequate, OC will still sometimes resort to both violence and intimidation on the one hand, and attempts to influence the state and media on the other. In line with his underlying commitment to avoid head-hunting when attempting to contain

OC, Vander Beken argues instead for a structural approach; authorities should attempt to alter market conditions so that OC is less able and tempted to take advantage of change (for a more detailed approach by Vander Beken and eleven other specialists see Vander Beken et al. 2006).

3.4   Problems with the various methods

By now it will be abundantly clear that, at our present stage of research and knowledge, we can only ever form a hazy picture of the scale of OC activity in any given jurisdiction because of numerous definitional, methodological and cultural problems and differences. It will also be clear that, unfortunately, there are problems with *all* the methods identified here for measuring the scale of crime generally, and OC in particular. We can begin our analysis of these by considering the problems with official statistics.

According to the EU's statistical office, comparing the crime rates between two or more states based on the absolute reported figures is potentially highly misleading, since they are impacted by many factors. These include different legal and criminal justice systems; different rates at which crimes are reported to the police and recorded by them; differences in the point at which crime is measured (for example, in one country it is the point at which a crime is reported to the police, whereas in another it is the point at which a suspect is identified); differences in the rules on how multiple offences are counted; and differences in the classification of offences included in the overall crime figures. Generally speaking, according to Eurostat, comparisons can only be made on the basis of *trends* rather than levels (for example, crime is increasing in Country A and decreasing or stable in Country B), and even then on the assumption that the basics of the crime recording system within a particular country remain relatively stable over time (Eurostat 2015a).

The problems outlined in the previous paragraph are compounded by the fact that the assumption of basic continuity in crime recording does not apply in all states. Thus some countries – including Georgia, Latvia and Lithuania in the 2000s – have changed the way in which they record and present crime statistics. While this has generally been a welcome development, in that the changes have been made to render crime statistics recording methods more directly comparable with those used in other countries, it has meant that the crime rates have looked *worse* in these countries than they previously did. The *actual* rates may not have changed much, if at all; but the perception that criminal activity has increased can be unsettling for local populations.

The EU is very aware of these problems of comparability, as it made clear in the European Council's Hague Programme (2004). It has since been working to standardise reporting methods, and declared in its 2009 Stockholm Programme that some progress had been made. But it still has a way to go. Together with the UNODC, and following a 2012 report (UNODC/UNECE Task Force on Crime Classification), the EU began piloting an "International Crime Classification System" in early 2014. This was based on the call in the 2012 report for five principles to be used in standardising crime reporting – exhaustiveness, structure, mutual exclusiveness, description, and progressive implementation. Moreover, the 2012 report argued that classification should be based on criminal acts/events, the target(s) of the act, the seriousness of the act, the intent of the perpetrator, the modus operandi of the act, the degree of completion of the act, the degree of co-responsibility of other persons involved in the act/event, the sex and age of victims and perpetrators, and the policy area of the act/event (UNODC/UNECE Task Force on Crime Classification 2012: 5). The pilot study was scheduled for completion by the end of 2014; the outcome is considered in the conclusions to this chapter.

Interpol is also very conscious of the problems of non-comparability of crime statistics. A clear symbol of this is the fact that it stopped publishing cross-polity data in the early-2000s (it had begun to do so in 1950), precisely because such data could be and often were seriously misinterpreted. For instance, if one were to compare the overall crime rates (generally, not specifically for OC) in Sweden and Indonesia at the end of the 1990s, it would appear that the former had a crime rate more than 216 times higher than the latter! Anyone who has visited these two countries would find that statistic questionable.

But formal differences in states' reporting of crime are not the only reason why official statistics have to be treated at least cautiously, if not with a pinch of salt! There are also many *informal* reasons for substantial differences in the reported crime rates in different countries. One of the less well-known ones is that the propensity of citizens to insure their property can affect crime reporting. In countries in which a high percentage of citizens insure most of their property, thefts will be more frequently reported to the police, since the victims will need an official record from the latter to present to their insurance companies for compensation. It should be clear that, because of this, more affluent countries may *appear* to have higher theft rates than less affluent ones, whereas in fact there might be more thefts per head of population in the latter. Another explanatory factor is the average level of education in a society; for various reasons, including confidence in completing reports of a crime, better educated people are more likely to report crimes than less well educated ones. Even communication technologies can impact upon crime reporting; in poor villages in developing countries, there may be no ready means of reporting a theft to a police station that might be located many kilometers away, so that the crime goes unreported. While many of the points identified in this paragraph refer to crime reporting generally, the reader will recall that OC data are often included in broader categories of crime, rather than being disaggregated.

However, perhaps the most significant informal factor is the reporting culture. For instance, citizens, including businesspeople, may decide not to report OC activity because of fear of retribution from gangs or that the police are colluding with these gangs. In many countries, citizens may have little confidence that the law enforcement authorities can or will do anything about their reports anyway. On the other hand, they may be concerned that reporting OC activity will mean they can no longer secure their supplies of illicit drugs, cheap cigarettes, cheap product supplies (in the case of businesses), and so on. Moreover, there is a strong tradition in some cultures of addressing problems – even criminal acts – without recourse to the state.

The reporting culture of the general public is not the only culture that helps to explain widely divergent reporting rates. Another is the culture of the law enforcement agencies themselves. As noted briefly above, some agencies will mendaciously over-report (that is, exaggerate) the number of crimes, often in the hope that this will result in additional funding from the government. Conversely, they will sometimes under-report for various reasons. A major one is that they are keen to minimise the gap between reported and solved crimes in order to appear more efficient than they really are. They may also under-report because of corruption; instead of issuing a fine to someone as they should, they prefer to take a bribe in return for not reporting the crime.

Government agencies and politicians also sometimes either consciously or unwittingly present highly misleading crime statistics to the general public. Thus politicians, especially during an election campaign, may either deliberately exaggerate (for example, if they are in opposition and want to enhance their electoral prospects by promising to clamp down on crime, including OC) or downplay (if they are currently in power) the crime statistics for political propaganda purposes. In other cases, the authorities are not deliberately publishing incorrect statistics, but have been misled by those reporting to them, such as the police, for reasons explained in the previous paragraph.

In addition to cultural problems, structural issues also help to explain why the reported incidence of OC activity can be well below the actual incidence. One is the problem of witness protection schemes. Studies have shown that the fate of witnesses who testify against criminal organisations often proves to be worse than that of those being accused – though it must be noted that the largest group of witnesses against OCGs is criminals themselves. Such witnesses sometimes have to change their identities, move to another town or country, and give up their network of friends and sometimes even their families (Fyfe and Sheptycki 2005; Bąkowski 2013b). It is hardly surprising that few are willing to testify against OC, and thereby increase conviction rates, in such a situation.

Because of the structural and cultural reasons identified – and our list is far from exhaustive – specialists such as Jan van Dijk have argued that crime statistics, which usually include OC statistics, bear little relationship to the actual experience of criminal victimisation. In his 2007 article (p. 25) already cited, the Dutch criminologist observes that "The number of crimes recorded by the police bears hardly any relationship to the ICVS-based measure of crime." But to compound the confusion, van Dijk goes on to argue that "The perceived prevalence of organized crime and the overall ICVS rates of victimization by common crime were found to be unrelated" (van Dijk 2007: 45). In short, he is suggesting that we cannot make inferences about the scale of OC on the basis of general crime statistics.

What of the crime threat assessments? Are they any better than victim surveys? Andries Zoutendijk (2010) argues that these new methodologies inadequately define key terms, such as organised crime and threat, and provide inadequate detail in most cases to ensure reliability and validity (see too von Lampe 2004). Natasha Tusikov (2012) argues that scholarly assessments of OC have tended to place insufficient emphasis on how law enforcement agencies conceptualise and measure the harm done by OC, and how such agencies use their assessments to set their priorities in combating OC. Her own preference is for OC to be measured in terms of the harm it does. Hers was not the first call for more emphasis on measurement in terms of the harm done, and a number of law enforcement agencies have engaged in it (Vander Beken et al. 2006: 56–104). But Tusikov maintains that such methods need further development and refinement. Citing examples from Australia, the Netherlands and the UK, she argues that the methods are often seriously flawed and opaque, and can result in inappropriate political interference in law enforcement agencies' attempts to address the OC problem. Tusikov acknowledges that an improvement in such methodologies requires clarity of definitions, but argues that this is a better way of measuring the nature and scale of OC, and that it would be a more appropriate way of determining suitable penalties for criminals. According to her comparative research, the best existing approach along these lines is that of the UK's National Policing Improvement Agency.

3.5   Conclusions

It will by now be clear that measuring OC is fraught with difficulties (see further Hobbs and Antonopoulos 2014). This is particularly true of TOC: as Cindy Hill (2005: 55) maintains, "an accurate assessment of the scale of transnational crime cannot be made. That is not to say that transnational crime cannot be measured". It is, rather, that our current measurement techniques are much less than perfect, in part because, in the case of TOC, different domestic jurisdictions use different definitions of criminal activities and OCGs.

This particular problem of definition may in future become less salient. The pilot study run by the UNODC and the EU in 2014 resulted in the publication in March 2015 of the first version of an *International Classification of Crime for Statistical Purposes (ICCS)* (UNODC 2015a). At the time of writing, the UNODC was requesting feedback on this report. While it could still take many years for this to be finalised, and then for a majority of states to adopt the standard approach to criminal (including OC) definitions and statistics advocated, a major step forward has now been taken.

Unfortunately, standardising definitions, assuming this does happen, will not in itself overcome the problem of different reporting cultures. But unless we believe that (T)OC will simply fade away – an extremely naïve assumption – we must continue to refine our methods, and hope that respondents will become less reluctant to answer sensitive questions, that law enforcement agencies will be more open and systematic in their reporting, and so on.

Despite the problems involved in measuring (T)OC in statistical terms, it is also clear from this chapter that the trend in measurement techniques is now away from examining particular gangs and even public or business perceptions and experiences, and towards an assessment of the perceptions – especially those of the police and market analysts – of the types of areas in which (T)OC is most likely to operate and develop. This is basically a risk-assessment approach, and is based on the assumption that OC is in essence just another form of enterprise – a market-oriented activity.

Yet it is far from obvious that we have to choose one or other of these various methods. The best approach is to combine as many methods as possible, to "multi-angulate", if we are to form a more precise picture of the nature and scale of OC in particular contexts. This multi-method approach is the best for what we most need from attempts at measurement, *viz.* devising methods and policies for combating it.

4   Major structured TOC groupings

A study of OC that considered it only in terms of abstract concepts, theories and generalisations could be dry and one-sided. This chapter therefore provides colour to the analysis by examining concrete examples of major TOC gangs and the types of activity in which they engage. It focuses on several of the best-known organisations, namely the Sicilian Mafia, the Chinese Triads, the Japanese Yakuza, the Russian "Mafiya", Mexican drug cartels and "Biker" gangs. To facilitate comparison across two or more groups by readers wishing to do so, a similar format – distinctive features; history; style and estimated size; activities; transnationalisation – has been adopted for each group's analysis. A final introductory comment is that the chapter focuses on more traditional OC formations, since the amorphous and constantly mutating nature of many more recent groups, especially those engaged in cybercrime, does not readily lend itself to structured description (though for sophisticated analyses of more amorphous OC activity from a "network analysis" perspective see Morselli 2005, 2010, 2014).

4.1   The Sicilian Mafia

In Anglophone countries, the best-known OC grouping is the Mafia. This originated in Sicily, though many members of the Mafia – *mafiosi* – migrated to the USA in the nineteenth and early twentieth centuries; a common convention is to call the Sicilian-based organisation the Mafia, and its American offshoot La Cosa Nostra (lit. "Our Thing" or "Our Business", depending on the translation) or LCN. The Mafia is in fact only one of four major criminal groupings in Italy, all of which are based in the South: the other three are the Naples-based Camorra, which is the oldest of these groups (see Behan 1996; Saviano 2007); the Calabrian 'Ndrangheta (see Nuzzi and Antonelli 2012; Serenata 2014), and the much more recently established Puglia-based Sacra Corona Unita (see Serenata 2014). There is also a less well-known second OCG based in Sicily, the Stidda.

There is no agreement on the origin of the term "Mafia". Although not widely accepted nowadays, two acronyms were at one time popular explanations. The first is "Morte alla Francia, Italia anela" (Italy yearns for death to France); Sicily had been under the Bourbons 1816–60, thus explaining the hostility to France – although some have argued that the term dates from a much earlier period of French domination, in the thirteenth century (Schram and Tibbetts 2014: 357). The second is "Mazzini autorizza furti, incendi, avvelenamenti" (Mazzini authorises theft, arson, poisoning). Giuseppe Mazzini was a nineteenth century political activist who advocated the unification of the numerous Italian states into what became the Kingdom of Italy in 1861. But many Southerners, including many Sicilians, were opposed to unification and the violence used by some of its advocates; this would help to explain the hostility to Mazzini. A third – and nowadays more popular – explanation is that the word derives from the name of a Sicilian witch, and signifies boldness and ambition (Hess 1998: 1); this is broadly in line with the suggestion that it derives from the masculine noun *mafiusu*, which referred in nineteenth century Sicily to either a courageous or a bullying male (Gambetta 1993: 136). Finally, some argue that the word derives from Arabic, either from *mahias/mahyas* (a brave or bragging man) or from *Ma-afir* (the name of the Arab tribe that ruled Palermo in the ninth and tenth centuries) or from *muhafiz* (protector or guardian).

Some of the terms originally associated with the Mafia are now commonly used in discussions about OC generally – and even beyond; the best examples are *omertà* (a code of silence, often also used in relation to corrupt police units) and either *pizzo or pizzu* (literally meaning "beak", but in this context meaning a protection payment).

Compared with most criminal organisations, the Mafia is a strongly "family"-based syndicate – though the term families here does not necessarily imply close blood relations – and has a strict family-oriented code. For instance, while it is commonly known that the Mafia will usually care for the immediate family of one of its members killed or imprisoned, it is less well known that *mafiosi* can be expelled for having extra-marital affairs. Its traditionalism – and in many ways its sexism – largely explains why in principle only men can join the organisation, though women have in recent times occasionally been permitted to take over the work of their husband if the latter has been incapacitated.

Despite its strict code of morality vis-à-vis the family, the Mafia has a number of traits that are by most criteria highly immoral. One is the initiation rite of passage; this typically involves a would-be member having to kill someone to prove their commitment to the cause, which partly explains the high number of murders committed by the Mafia. The officially recorded number of Mafia homicides in Sicily alone 1990–2011 was almost 1200, while the total number attributed to the three largest Italian OC syndicates – the Camorra, 'Ndrangheta and the Mafia itself – combined over the same period was almost 4000 (Paoli 2014b: 137).

A final introductory point is that, as noted in Chapter 1, the term mafia, derived from the original Mafia, is used by many to refer to a subsection of OCGs that has direct connections with politics. In 2013, the Italian Supreme Court of Cassation concluded that former prime minister Silvio Berlusconi had had business connections with the Mafia for some two decades, for example (Day 2014).

4.1.1   History

Just as the origin of the term "mafia" is disputed, so the origin of the organisation itself is unclear. It had certainly emerged by the middle of the nineteenth century. While some maintain that the term dates from either the ninth or the thirteenth centuries (Schram and Tibbetts 2014: 357), most now accept that the organisation that became the modern Mafia began to develop as the transition from feudalism in Sicily, which began in 1812, got underway. Many new landowners sought "protection" of their property rights, which was rarely supplied by the Sicilian authorities; the Mafia emerged to provide such protection. It was based in and around the Sicilian capital of Palermo, and was rarely seen in the east of the island.

It seems that from its earliest days, the Mafia was closely involved with politics. During the Fascist era (early-1920s to 1943), however, these political links were largely broken, and the state's clampdown on OC led to a new wave of Mafia emigration to the USA. But following the collapse of Mussolini's regime, the Italian Mafia began to consolidate and involve itself in politics once again. Like OC in many countries, the Mafia was clearly to the right of the political spectrum and hostile to the main left-of-centre party in those days, the Italian Communist Party.

During the 1950s and the 1960s, the Mafia was closely involved with the construction industry in Sicily, particularly in Palermo. But the 1960s also witnessed increasing warfare between different Mafia gangs, and the main attempt to end this, via the Sicilian Mafia Commission – comprising senior Mafiosi from different families – failed miserably. The 1970s witnessed an improvement in the situation. Mafia families now found a lucrative market for smuggled cigarettes, but also for heroin, which it began to produce and traffic, mainly to the USA. Unfortunately, the calm was short-lived, and by the 1980s, internal warfare had broken out again. It was also in the 1980s that the so-called "maxi-trial" of almost 500 Mafiosi was held in Palermo from early 1986 to late 1987. Partly in response to this clampdown by the state – 360 Mafiosi were convicted – the Mafia began assassinating judges and other law enforcement officers in what is sometimes described as OC terrorism. The most famous cases were the assassinations of anti-mafia judges Paolo Borsellino and Giovanni Falcone in 1992, after they had proven to be hardliners against Mafiosi appealing their maxi-trial sentences.

The murders of Borsellino and Falcone proved to be a turning point, and the authorities now clamped down heavily again on the Mafia, resulting in a weakening of this criminal organisation. By the 2000s, it was claimed that the Mafia was even transferring some its business to other OC groupings, including its cocaine dealing to the 'Ndrangheta. Nevertheless, and despite many more arrests and imprisonments of Mafiosi during the twenty-first century, the Mafia has continued to operate, and there have been official reports since at least 2012 that it has linked up with Mexican drug syndicates to import cocaine into Europe via the port of Palermo (Capo 2012).

4.1.2   Style and estimated size

The Mafia has a very traditional hierarchical (pyramidal) structure: at the top is the *capo* (head), below whom are "soldiers" and associates. In the past, one of the Mafia's salient features has been strict adherence to its code, including the *omertà*. But this has been breaking down since the 1980s, as a number of Mafia members have acted as informants (*pentiti*). For instance, before and during the maxi-trial of 1986–7, the evidence provided by Tommaso Buscetta, who broke the code of silence in 1984 and is usually seen as the first of the Mafia informants to provide really detailed information on the workings of the organisation, was crucial. Some idea of just how widespread this practice has become is conveyed by the fact that there were 1214 *pentiti* under witness protection schemes in 1996, and 1093 in 2011 (Paoli 2014b: 136).

While it is not possible to provide definitive data on the scale of the Sicilian Mafia, it is believed to comprise approximately 150 "families" or clans (Paoli 2014b: 124 – citing a 2012 official Italian Ministry of the Interior source).

4.1.3 Activities

Traditionally, the Mafia was involved primarily in protection. It still engages in this – as emphasised by Diego Gambetta (1993) in his classic analysis of the Mafia – which assumes various forms. For instance, the Mafia often acts as a "guarantor" between two agents engaged in a deal with each other that involves illegal activity. In other words, the Mafia ensures that both sides fulfil their part of an agreed bargain in cases where neither partner would want to report non-fulfilment by the other to law enforcement authorities. A second form of protection is offered to businesses that want to minimise competition from other companies; the latter will sometimes be threatened with violence if they seek to compete with the former in a given market.

In addition to protection, drug trafficking had by the second half of the twentieth century become another major activity of the Mafia. Mafiosi also often facilitate smuggling operations, though they rarely engage in this directly themselves. Conversely, as part of their code of honour, Mafiosi are not supposed to engage in either theft or kidnapping – a rule that is sometimes broken, however. Finally, loan sharking has become a major activity of the Mafia. There are claims that the Mafia has in recent years become the largest bank in Italy as a result of the Global Financial Crisis (GFC); many small business owners found it difficult to secure loans from the regular Italian banks in the general tightening of financial control that occurred post-2008, and so turned to the Mafia.

4.1.4 Transnationalisation

In the 1990s, Alison Jamieson (1995) noted that, while many had believed that Italian OC was so entrenched and locally-based that it was unlikely to develop into TOC, both the Mafia and other Italian OC groups had in fact been linking up with OC groups overseas, particularly for drug trafficking. This argument is in line with a much broader one about OC that was published at about the same time and is better known, Claire Sterling's (1994) notion of a *"pax mafiosa"* (mafia peace). According to this, the early-1990s saw a marked change in the nature of OC, with a substantial decline in turf wars, and the rapid expansion of cooperation between OC groupings in different countries (see also Freemantle 1995). While this thesis has been challenged (for example, Naylor 1995) and was certainly overstated, there is no question that the underlying development Sterling claimed to have identified has proven to be real enough. While turf wars still occur, these are mainly between groups within one country (that is, domestic disputes), and there is no contradiction between this fact and the notion that international collaboration has significantly increased since the beginning of the 1990s.

4.2   The Triads

It is widely believed that the world's largest OC syndicate is the Chinese Triads. Since China is the world's most populous country, with c. 1.3 billion inhabitants, this is on one level not surprising. But it has to be borne in mind that it is only relatively recently that the Triads have moved back into mainland (Communist) China; for many years, they were headquartered in Hong Kong, which even now has a population of only just over seven million. This makes the initial assumption less obvious. Moreover, it also has to be noted that the Triads are only one part of what we call Chinese OC; there is no question that the Triads themselves account for only a small percentage of the total OC membership. According to Plywaczewski (2002), Chinese OC was seen by many Western agencies during the 1990s as the No.1 TOC threat.

The origin of the name Triad is disputed. The dominant view is that the term was chosen to symbolise the threefold unity of the principal elements of existence – heaven, earth and humanity (Chin 2014: 220). Others maintain that it referred either to the founding of the organisation in the Three Rivers region, or to the three men said to have established it (Chu 2000: 13). In line with the argument in Chapter 1 about the differences between mafias and other types of OC, some branches of Chinese OC have developed close ties with the authorities, including politicians (Chin 2014: 229) – though hard evidence on this in the specific case of the Triads is thin (but see Vines 1998).

4.2.1   History

The history of the Triads has been traced back to the seventeenth century, at which time, according to many interpretations, it was primarily a political force; it was opposed to the Manchurian Qing dynasty that had come to power in China 1644, and was agitating to return an ethnically (Han) Chinese dynasty to power (Lintner 2002: 41–2). However, the Triads failed to bring about this change (the Qing dynasty did not collapse until 1911), and by the nineteenth century had begun to mutate from a political into an OC movement. According to Chu (2000: 12–13), by contrast, the Triads date from the 1760s, and were an OC syndicate offering protection right from the start; his analysis is compatible with the notion that the Triads were primarily involved in OC activity by the late-nineteenth or early-twentieth century, however.

Once it was separated from the rest of China and became a British Colony (1842), the Triads focused more on Hong Kong than on most of mainland China, though they retained an interest in the port city of Shanghai. After 1949, as mainland China came under Communist control, so the Triads focused increasingly on Hong Kong; like Stalin in the USSR and Mussolini in Italy, Mao Zedong was determined to eradicate OC in his country. Following Mao's death in 1976 and the rise to power of Deng Xiaoping, the situation slowly began to change. The new Communist leadership started to introduce major reform that gradually liberalised China's economy. By the 1990s and into the 2000s, OC had begun to spread in mainland China once again. This was not only in the form of the Triads, but also other so-called "Black" or "Dark" (the Chinese word *hei* can be translated either way) Societies. The latter had already been identified by the authorities in Shenzhen (a city very close to Hong Kong, but located in Communist China) in the early-1980s as a phenomenon that needed to be eradicated. The return of Hong Kong to Chinese control in 1997 and its semi-incorporation into mainland China was a further stimulus to the spread of OC into China.

But the Chinese authorities have sought to clamp down hard on OC, including the Triads, since the 1980s, with "strike hard" (*yanda*) anti-OC campaigns beginning in 1983 (Trevaskes 2010). Moreover, the central Chinese government's concern about the spread of violent OC activity was by 2000 so deep that, in an unprecedented move, they permitted Chinese law enforcement to link up with the USA's Drug

Enforcement Agency (DEA) (as well as Hong Kong law enforcement agencies) to monitor and then – in 2003 – bring down the Fujian-based "Four Untouchables" that was said to be responsible for trafficking heroin worth more than US$100 million between 2000 and 2003 (Drug Enforcement Administration 2003). The Chinese authorities have a reputation for resisting "interference" by foreign powers, especially the USA, so that this combined operation – codenamed City Lights – set a welcome precedent. This was especially so since earlier anti-drug trafficking cooperation had soured because of US criticism of China's use of torture to secure confessions.

4.2.2   Style and estimated size

Whereas the Triads used to be structured in a fairly rigid hierarchical way, with a Red Pole at the top, "49s" as the ordinary members, and Blue Lanterns as the recruits, they have in recent years become more relaxed and less code-oriented. Moreover, they have – like some other OC groupings – sought to engage increasingly with the licit economy, in what Roderic Broadhurst (2012) has called the "gentrification" of the Triads.

There are considerable differences in estimates of the size of the Triads. At one end of the spectrum is Lyman and Potter's (2015: 273) figure of more than 100,000, at the other end a figure of approximately 1.3 million members (Plywaczewski 2002). Much of this discrepancy is due to the fact that some analysts use a very broad definition of Triads, to include various Chinese OC groupings (for example, mainly North America-based Tongs; Fujian-based people smugglers known as Snakeheads; Taiwanese *jiaotou* – for a brief but valuable overview of the various groups see Chin 2014: 220–3), whereas others use a narrower approach, focusing explicitly on the Hong Kong-based Triads. One 1998 estimate of the latter suggests a broad membership of approximately 120,000 (Vines 1998), still a sizeable number.

4.2.3   Activities

The Triads have been involved in a wide range of activities, including drug trafficking, extortion/protection, prostitution, trafficking cultural relics, loan sharking and credit card fraud. Among their more unusual activities is pharmaceutical crime, including trafficking of often dangerous erectile dysfunction medication.

4.2.4   Transnationalisation

The Triads' main operational area outside China (including HK and Macao) was for a long time Europe. Although it seems that the 14K group has been operating in Amsterdam since the 1930s, there was Triad expansion to other parts of Europe in the 1950s. But the major period of expansion was the 1970s, as the growth in demand for illicit drugs that had emerged with the hippie generation of the 1960s showed no sign of decreasing; the Triads were keen to capitalise on this demand. In recent decades, however, there has been significant expansion of Triad activity, so that one analysis focusing on this trans-nationalisation by the early-2000s referred to its geographical spread as encompassing "Australia, Europe, Japan, Latin America, North America, Russia, South Africa and Southeast Asia" (Curtis et al. 2002: 19); since the authors excluded China, Hong Kong, Macao or Taiwan from their analysis, given their focus on transnationalisation, it seems that there were by the start of this century few places in the world in which Triads were not operating (see too Berry et al. 2003).

4.3   The Yakuza

Jointly with the Triads, Japan's Yakuza are Asia's best-known OCG. One of their distinguishing features is that they have until recently been far more open in their activities than most criminal organisations, having had shopfronts that openly acknowledged they were Yakuza "outlets". Another, briefly mentioned in Chapter 2, is that they tra-ditionally had much better relations with the general public than do most criminal organisations. This was largely because the Yakuza have on occasions greatly assisted ordinary Japanese affected by natural dis-asters, notably earthquakes; sometimes, the state's responses in such an emergency are not as rapid as they should be, because of bureau-cratic delays, whereas the Yakuza have proven themselves capable of very quick reactions. Nevertheless, public attitudes in Japan towards the Yakuza have been hardening – becoming more critical – since the 1990s.

Like the terms Mafia and Triads, the origin of the term Yakuza is dis-puted. The most common assumption is that it is a local Japanese dialect term for "893", an unlucky hand in a Japanese card game. The organisa-tion is known by various other names, including the *bōryokudan* (vio-lence group – a term favoured by Japanese law enforcement agencies) and *ninkyō dantai* (chivalrous organisations – a term preferred by Yakuza members themselves).

4.3.1 History

Most historians of the Yakuza trace their origins to the seventeenth century (the early Tokugawa era), though they emerged gradually from other organisations and formations. Although there is a common perception that the Yakuza derived from the Samurai warrior class, the dominant view among specialists nowadays is that they arose as a *reaction* to former Samurai warriors who were by the seventeenth century no longer a military class. By this time, though many had become administrators, other Samurai felt alienated because of having lost their martial role, and were wandering around Japan threatening townsfolk. The latter therefore formed groups to protect themselves, which in turn became the nucleus of the Yakuza. In this sense, the early Yakuza were somewhat akin to other OCGs, providing a form of protection (on the differing views on the origins of the Yakuza see Kaplan and Dubro 2012: 4–7).

Hill (2014: 234) has pointed out that nineteenth century illegal gambling organisations were the other antecedent to the modern Yakuza; this would explain the fact that the name for this OC grouping relates to a card game. Following the Meiji restoration (1868), the Japanese state sought to clamp down on these gambling organisations. But over time, the relationship changed dramatically, and by the 1920s, some right-wing politicians hired members of the Yakuza to quell labour unrest by force. The Yakuza were then again suppressed in the 1930s by the fascist regime. But they made a comeback after the Second World War, when they essentially ran the black markets at a time of widespread shortages. The law enforcement agencies began to clamp down heavily on the Yakuza in the 1960s, however, and membership declined. By the 1980s, the Yakuza had started to make a serious comeback, though another government clampdown from 1992 again reduced their influence, and they have never regained the position they had in the years following the Second World War.

4.3.2 Style and estimated size

Like the Mafia, the Yakuza are structured in a traditional hierarchical fashion; at the top of each grouping is a *kumi-cho* or *oyabun* (boss or father figure), below whom are six different levels down to the *jun-kosei-in* (Hill 2003: 65–6). As already noted, one of the distinctive features of the Yakuza has been their relative openness, though this has recently been changing. Like all of the OCGs considered in this chapter, the Yakuza comprise many subgroupings, the largest and best known of which is the Yamaguchi-gumi.

It is estimated that there were over 184,000 members of the Yakuza in the early-1960s. According to Japanese law enforcement agencies, this number had declined markedly to less than 87,000 members at the end of 1988, organised in 3197 groups; just under half of these groups were affiliated with one of the three national syndicates – the Yamaguchi-gumi, the Inagawa-kai and the Sumiyoshi-kai (Hill 2003: 63). Membership had declined slightly to approximately 78,600 members in 2010 (Hill 2014: 235), and has since dropped quite considerably to less than 60,000 by 2013. One major reason for this reduction is that the Yakuza have been ageing and not replacing former members with younger members at a rate that would maintain the organisation's size.

4.3.3 Activities

Like the Mafia, the Yakuza have a long history of engagement in protection rackets. They are also known to be active in illegal gambling, THB and prostitution. But one of the most interesting and contested aspects of the Yakuza's activity is their involvement in illicit drugs. There are allegations that, under a tacit agreement with the Japanese authorities, the Yakuza long agreed not to traffic heavy drugs such as cocaine and heroin, but to deal only in relatively lighter drugs, notably amphetamines (though not cannabis). The Yakuza's unusual stance on drugs has now gone one step further, with the three largest syndicates all declaring their opposition to them. The Yamaguchi-gumi has been proclaiming its opposition since as early as 1963, while in 2014, as part of a drive to recruit new members, it developed a website that emphasises its opposition to drugs, including amphetamines and the more dangerous methamphetamines. However, Kaplan and Dubro (2012) maintain that there is a significant difference between the Yakuza's statements and their practice, and that they have been heavily involved in drug trafficking in recent decades.

4.3.4 Transnationalisation

For much of the twentieth century, it was assumed in the West that the Yakuza were very focused on Japan. This was always a misconception. The Yakuza had become active in several other Asian states in the 1920s, although this declined in the 1930s. But they became very active again in Asia in the 1960s, and then moved further afield – to Latin America, Europe, Australia and then North America (having already established themselves much earlier in Hawaii) – by the 1980s (for details see Kaplan and Dubro 2012: 221–323). The 1992 clampdown in Japan only intensified this transnationalisation process.

4.4   The Russian "Mafiya"

Although many commentators use a russified version of the Sicilian term to describe Russian organised crime, this is potentially misleading. First, there are at least two clear strands in Russian organised crime – on the one hand the more traditional "thieves-in-law" (*vory v zakone*, sometimes translated as "thieves living by the code"), whose origins can be traced back to the 1920s, and on the other the various new gangs that emerged in the 1990s. Whereas the former bear some resemblance to the Sicilian Mafia, the latter have little in common with the Italian organisation, although their 1990s activities have been compared with the latter's in providing contract protection in the context of a weak state (Leitzel 1995: 43; Williams 1997b: 5–6). For instance, the thieves-in-law have a strict 13-point code of behaviour (Varese 2001: 150–6) and a relatively rigid hierarchy, whereas the new generation of Russian criminal organisations is much more fluid and less disciplined. Second, Russian OC is not typically based on "family" or clan ties, unlike the Mafia. Third, the traditional groups at least – the thieves-in-law – were committed via their code to avoiding all forms of involvement in politics, whereas some members of the new gangs have had close connections with political elites. Finally, the thieves-in-law code forbids *vory* from using violence in their activities, whereas violence was a notable feature of the new brand of Russian OC. These significant differences notwithstanding, as long as the russified spelling is used so as to distinguish Russian OC from its Sicilian and US (LCN) counterparts, the fact that the term "mafiya" is now in such common usage suggests it can be used here.

An indication of how seriously Russian OC has been taken outside Russia is the fact that in May 1996, the heads of both the CIA (John Deutch) and the FBI (Louis Freeh) warned the US Congress that Russian OC and corruption were undermining the Russian system, and could pose a threat to the USA. A year later, another senior security official,

William Webster (with others – 1997: 45), claimed that "Corruption of the official Russian bureaucracy poses, in many ways, the most serious threat to the interests of the United States and other countries." Among the potential corruptors was OC. The claimed severity of the threat was a gross exaggeration. But in terms of the dangers posed to Russia itself, President Boris Yeltsin claimed in February 1993 that "Organised crime has become a direct threat to Russia's strategic interests and national security" (Talalayev 1993).

4.4.1 History

Although there is limited evidence of OC in the Russian Empire in the period before the Bolshevik (Communist) Revolution of October 1917, such as groups of horse thieves and beggars (Rawlinson 1997: 36–7, 39–40; Varese 2001: 160–6), the *vory v zakone* were a product of the Soviet era. They arose in the Soviet prison camps, and developed their own microcosm, the so-called "thieves world". Although the totalitarian dictator Stalin sought to eradicate OC, the thieves-in-law managed to survive this period. In fact, one of the most significant dangers to the *vory* in the late-1940s was themselves, as they split into two groupings and fought the so-called "bitches' war". One group comprised thieves who had decided to fight for their country in what the Russians call the "Great Patriotic War" (that is, the Second World War); these thieves were released from prison to become soldiers, and were called "bitches" (*suki*) by those thieves who preferred to remain in their prison camps than fight for the Soviet authorities. Many "bitches" began engaging in criminal activity again after the war; upon their return to prison, they were treated with contempt by the *vory* who had refused to cooperate with the Soviet authorities.

The shortages of consumer goods, both durable and non-durable, that typified the Soviet economic system meant that the thieves-in-law were able to play a role in the running of a black market after the death of Stalin (1953), although the "bitches' war" led to a marked decline in the number of *vory* by the end of the 1950s. But the whole OC situation changed in the 1990s. The USSR finally collapsed in December 1991, and there was near chaos for much of the rest of the decade. In this context, new OC groupings emerged, most of which had little time for the strict code of the *vory*. Gang warfare erupted between both the *vory* and the newcomers, and among the latter themselves.

A salient feature of the new OC groupings in the 1990s was the significant role played by former KGB officers. As happened in many other post-communist states, the new Russian authorities were anxious to distance themselves from the former system, and as a concrete symbol of this substantially downgraded and downsized the secret police. Many unemployed former KGB officers felt alienated from the new system, and so were more easily enticed into a life of crime than they would otherwise have been. Such former officers were attractive to OCGs for a number of reasons: they were well trained in the use of weapons, often had access to such weapons, were not squeamish about using violence, and often still had (potentially corruptible) insider contacts in the law enforcement agencies and knowledge of how these units operated, including how they worked to combat OC.

The OC situation in Russia has been calmer in the 2000s than it was during the 1990s. This is partly because of the decline of the role of the *vory* and the moves taken by other groups into the more legal economy. But another factor is that corrupt police officers have in some cases replaced OC gangs, especially in running protection rackets. The changes are sufficiently marked for one of the leading analysts of Russian OC to refer to the "extinction" of the Russian mafia, and to claim that the phenomenon had been a "one-generation" one (Volkov 2014: esp. 159). This might be an overly optimistic or premature assessment, however. While there can be no question that Russian OC is less violent and less visible in Russia than it was in the 1990s, Russians figure prominently in the rapidly growing field of global cybercrime (Glenny 2011; NCA 2015: 18).

4.4.2   Style and estimated size

As already noted, the style of Russian OC is diverse, ranging from the traditional, code-oriented *vory v zakone* through to the newer, less structured gangs, and arguably even to the so-called oligarchs (in other words, extremely wealthy Russians who have made their fortunes in ways some consider at least illicit, if not illegal).

Obtaining accurate statistics on the size of Russian OC is just as problematic as it is for other OC groupings. Joseph Serio (2008) makes a convincing argument that the data are often contradictory and definitely confusing; however, he also notes that both the number of gangs and the number of people involved almost certainly *declined* in the 2000s. Official figures on the thieves-in-law suggest that this traditional branch of Russian OC has never been large in the post-Soviet era, with a maximum number in Russia of 740 in 1994 (Varese 2001: 167–8). In 2013, the Russian Ministry of the Interior estimated that there were only some 500 thieves-in-law left, and that most of these were not Russian anyway, but Georgian. Thus, while it is too early to refer to the "extinction" of OC in Russia, some branches of it are numerically small.

4.4.3   Activities

Russian OCGs have engaged in a wide range of criminal activities, including THB. But two areas to single out are their significant involvement in cybercrime, and their alleged smuggling of nuclear materials during the 1990s. Quite how widespread the latter was is highly disputed. Moreover, it seems likely that had they really been engaging in such smuggling to any significant extent, there would by now have been evidence of it in the form of dirty bombs. This said, the allegations that some materials were actually sold to state authorities (for example, in Pakistan) are less easily dismissed than the suggestion that the Russian mafiya was selling such materials to non-state terrorist groups. Certainly, the Russian Federal Security Service (FSB) claimed in mid-2002 that OC groups were increasing their attempts to sell components for both nuclear and chemical weapons, though it was unclear who the potential customers were.

4.4.4   Transnationalisation

According to many analysts, the new version of Russian OC became ubiquitous in the 1990s, but has been a particular problem in the US and Israel. Regarding the former, the issue was considered sufficiently serious by the early-1990s that a "Tri-State Joint Soviet-Emigré Organized Crime Project" was established in 1992 by the US states of New York, New Jersey and Pennsylvania specifically to investigate and address it. The project's final report concluded that, while there was certainly a problem with "crimes of a highly organised and complex kind" being committed by Russians and other émigrés from the former USSR, there was no evidence of major Russian crime groups in the US organised in a highly structured way and operating as a mafia. Rather, teams of specialists from the former Soviet Union were often brought together to commit specific crimes (Finckenauer and Waring 1998a). While this phenomenon might not constitute a mafia in its strict sense, such a description could apply to much of what we nowadays see as the new, more loosely networked forms of OC in so many parts of the world (for further analyses of the transnationalisation of Russian and post-Soviet OC see Part 5 of Galeotti 2002).

4.5 Mexican drug cartels

From the 1970s to the 1990s, the best-known Latin American OCGs were the Colombian drug cartels. But a concerted effort by the Colombian and US authorities led to the near decimation of these; they had been major suppliers of cocaine to the USA (and elsewhere), which explains the American involvement. Thus both of the two most famous cartels – the Medellín, headed by the notorious "King of Cocaine" Pablo Escobar, and the Cali – had been essentially destroyed by the mid-1990s. While there were still large and powerful drug gangs operating in and from Colombia until 2012, when the Norte del Valle Cartel was dismantled by Colombian and US authorities, Mexico has in recent years become the number one centre for drug trafficking in the Americas.

An indication of how seriously the USA has treated the Sinaloa cartel – one of Mexico's most infamous – is that its head until his arrest in February 2014, Joaquín "El Chapo" ("Shorty") Guzmán Loera, was in 2013 named "public enemy number one" by the Chicago city authorities. Another sign of his perceived significance in contemporary OC is that Guzmán has been described by CNN as the "the first [crime boss] to develop a truly global narcotics and criminal network" (Meacham 2014), and by *Forbes* magazine in February 2014 as the "world's most notorious and powerful drug lord" (for a detailed analysis of Guzmán and his operations see Hernández 2013).

Like so many other OC groupings analysed in this chapter, an important source of members of many of the Mexican cartels is disillusioned former soldiers or police officers; further details are provided in the conclusions to this chapter.

4.5.1 History

Although crime gangs had existed in parts of Mexico for centuries, the modern drug cartels have been traced back to the early twentieth century. In 1914, the US passed the Harrison Narcotics Act – one of the earliest pieces of legislation prohibiting the sale or use of mainly opiate drugs – which has been seen by Grillo (2011) as having encouraged the illicit growing of opium poppies in neighbouring Mexico; prohibition of products tends to substantially increase their price (and profitability), and thus to encourage OC. The production was based mainly in the Sierra Madre Occidental, especially the coastal state of Sinaloa, which has been compared to Sicily in terms of its criminality. In those early days, the trafficking was conducted primarily by Chinese immigrants; but this changed in the 1930s, as Mexicans took over the business from the Chinese, often violently.

But Mexican drug trafficking was still a relatively small business. There was some growth in the 1960s and 1970s, as Americans dramatically increased their consumption of recreational drugs. However, the real boost to the contemporary role of the Mexican drug cartels came in the 1990s. With the decimation of their two major cartels, the Colombians ceased to be the major Latin American player and were replaced by the Mexicans.

4.5.2   Style and estimated size

Nowadays, perhaps the most salient aspect of the Mexican drug cartels is their extreme violence, with the Los Zetas group being one of the most bloodthirsty. The Sinaloa (or Pacific) drug cartel, founded in 1989 and widely considered to be the world's most powerful drug trafficking syndicate, has a hit squad, Los Ántrax – allegedly now headed by a woman, Claudia Ochoa Félix, although she has publicly denied this – that has been accused of committing numerous murders. A preferred method of some cartels is decapitation, which they often publicise on the Internet; it is not only terrorist groups such as IS that engage in this gruesome and primitive practice. The sheer scale of the killing is shocking. According to the Mexican authorities, there were more than 56,000 drug-related murders between 2001 and 2011, with more than 15,000 being carried out in 2010 alone (Medel and Thoumi 2014: 211); by 2014, the total for the period 2006–14 was approximately 80,000 (Wilson 2014). And there is no end in sight to the violence: in May 2015, a major battle between the police and a relatively new drug cartel, the Jalisco New Generation, had resulted in 43 deaths (42 gang members and one police officer).

Unfortunately, there are no official statistics on the number of criminals involved in the Mexican drug cartels. However, the number is clearly in the thousands.

4.5.3   Activities

Unlike most of the OC groupings considered in this chapter, the Mexicans have essentially focused on just one type of OC activity, the manufacture and trafficking of drugs; while the Los Zetas cartel, for example, has also engaged in other activities such as extortion and protection rackets, these are generally of secondary importance. Other OCGs do exist in Mexico and focus on activities such as people smuggling into the US; but the drug cartels remain specialised. This said, they have changed their primary focus in terms of the drugs they traffic. Until the mid-1990s, Mexican gangs were primarily dealing in marijuana and heroin; since that time, the focus has switched to the far more profitable cocaine.

4.5.4   Transnationalisation

While Mexican drug cartels have traditionally operated in the Americas – both Latin and North, especially the USA – they have in recent years begun to move further afield. In particular, groups such as the Sinaloa Cartel have been using Guinea-Bissau – sometimes called the world's first "narco-state" – and other fragile West African states as conduits for trafficking cocaine into Europe. In fact, the Sinaloa Cartel is said to have connections stretching right across the globe to Australia (Bender 2014).

4.6   "Biker" (outlaw motorcycle) gangs

In recent decades, a very visible form of criminal organisation in many countries of the Western world has been outlaw motorcycle gangs (OMCGs). These typically ride "cruiser" motorcycles and proudly display their affiliation to their particular gang on the backs of their black leather jackets, and often via tattoos. They often claim to be freer than other people, and typically appear to have little respect for government authorities.

From their names alone (apart from the Comancheros, who are named after nineteenth century traders), it is clear that these gangs have adopted monikers that identify them as macho outsiders – "Outlaws", "Bandidos", "Hells Angels", and so on. They are sometimes referred to as "one-percenters", a term said by some to have been coined by the American Motorcyclist Association (AMA), which allegedly argued in the late-1940s that 99 per cent of American motorcyclists are law-abiding, implying that the remaining one per cent were not; the AMA has denied making such a statement, however, and many US OMCGs now claim they adopted the term themselves.

In Australia, "bikies" (this, rather than bikers, is the Australian term) have been described as "the country's first nationwide crime syndicate" (Marsden and Sher 2006: 3). In a manner somewhat akin to that of many of the newer OCGs in Central and Eastern Europe, some of these gangs are alleged to be actively recruiting former members of the military (in CEE it is primarily former members of the internal security police, though ex-soldiers are another important source of recruits) who have served in conflict zones (Silvester 2015), in part because of their experience with weapons and their battle-toughened attitudes towards violence.

Like so many other OCGs, individual gangs that fall under the umbrella term of "US bikers" or "Australian bikies" are often in conflict with each other, and many of the murders committed by members of OMCGs are of members of other gangs. In perhaps the most famous Australian case of such internecine warfare, the so-called Battle of Milperra (1984; Milperra is a suburb of Sydney) between members of the Comancheros and Bandidos gangs, seven people were killed, including a seven-year-old girl; the "battle" resulted in 21 bikies receiving prison sentences of at least seven years. There has also been significant in-fighting among Canadian OMCGs, notably during the so-called Quebec Biker War of 1994–2002.

Some OMCGs have in recent times been attempting to improve their public image – for instance by claiming to be engaged in charity work. A concrete example is of the Bandidos in Australia, who in 2014 publicised a bike run they were organising as designed to raise money for a hospital (Chambers 2014). But the AMA has criticised the presence of OMCGs at American charity events, claiming that their negative image discourages potential donors from making contributions.

4.6.1 History

The best-known – though not oldest – outlaw motorcycle gang is the US-based Hells Angels, formed in California in 1948, shortly after the end of the Second World War. According to its own website, it became "international" in 1961, when a branch was established in New Zealand

– though the major expansion to other parts of the world occurred from the end of the 1960s. The dates of the establishment of other major clubs in the Anglophone world are as follows: Outlaws (1935), Pagans (1959), Bandidos (1966), Sons of Silence (1966), Comancheros (1968) and Rebels (1969). Some of the gangs that were formed in the 1960s and that grew in the 1970s included many veterans of the Vietnam War (for a detailed analysis of the history of OCMGs see Lauchs et al. 2015: 7–21; see too Barker 2014, primarily on US OMCGs, and Veno 2009 on Australian bikies).

4.6.2   Style and estimated size

Like most traditional OC groupings, a salient feature of the bikies is their penchant for violence. Again like so many other OCGs, most OMMGs are structured hierarchically – with a president, treasurer, secretary, road captain, sergeant-at-arms, and full members (a.k.a. "patched" members) – and tend to enforce military-style discipline among their members (Lauchs et al. 2015). On the other hand, OMCGs tend to be much more visible than some other OC groupings, but also less involved in politics.

It is difficult to provide even a guesstimate of the global membership number of the bikies, given their spread now to so many countries. One law enforcement estimate of the global scale of the Hells Angels is 2000 members, while the US Department of Justice estimated the global membership (in 14 countries) of the Bandidos as 2000–2500 and of the Outlaws (in 13 countries) as 1700 (Barker 2014: 26–30), all of which seem relatively small numbers. But the Australian Crime Commission identified some 6000 Australian bikies as of 2013. If this is the figure in Australia alone, there can be no doubt that global membership of all OMCGs is in the tens of thousands.

4.6.3   Activities

OMCGs engage in various kinds of criminal activity, but are best known for their involvement in the trafficking of recreational drugs – nowadays, especially methamphetamines – and counterfeit pharmaceuticals. Two other areas of OC several OMCGs appear to have become increasingly involved in is weapons trafficking and extortion.

4.6.4 Transnationalisation

While the internationalisation of OMCGs can be traced back to the 1960s, the process has intensified since the 1990s; biker gangs can now be found in all continents. Early in 2015, it was claimed by a senior law enforcement officer that Victoria, Australia, was being targeted by international OMCGs because of the hugely inflated prices Australian recreational drug users were prepared to pay for methamphetamines – between A\$220,000 and A\$300,000 per kilo, compared with an average of A\$5,600 in the US (Silvester 2015).

4.7 Conclusions

Details of many other traditional OCGs could be provided here. For instance, Albania has been described as the "new Colombia of Europe", and Albanian OCGs as the world's new number one heroin dealers (Michaletos 2007 and 2012). Albanian OC is also yet another example of the rigidly hierarchical structure so typical of traditional OCGs, and is code-based (Arsovska 2006). It has played a major role in THB, especially within Europe, and has a reputation for extreme violence (Europol 2011: 30) and misogyny. Its roots can be traced back to the sixteenth century, thus even further than those of other groups considered here – and many of its members have a secret service or paramilitary background. But space limitations prevent exploration of other OCGs.

The information contained in his chapter mostly makes for depressing reading. The deliberate violence used by these groups is sickening, even if it appears to be in decline in some cases. This is one reason why comparisons with corporate ("upperworld") crime should not be exaggerated.

There are discernible patterns across many of the groups. For instance, major transition in a country often engenders new OC groupings, or leads to a major growth in old ones; this has been shown here in the case of Russia, but also applies to countries such as Albania, Bulgaria, Lithuania, Romania and Serbia.

Another clear pattern to emerge from comparison of OC in such transition states is that an important source of new members for gangs is former members of the security (secret) police, and to some extent former members of the military. But this is not peculiar to transition states. A major source of recruits into some American biker gangs is former US marines, while the very violent Los Zetas Cartel in Mexico started life at the end of the 1990s as a group of deserters from the army's elite "Mobile Air Group of Special Forces" that operated as the armed wing of the Gulf Cartel (they left the Gulf Cartel in 2010 to form their own). Like their peers in other countries, not only are such former soldiers or secret service police officers well trained in the use of weapons, but many have been at least partly desensitised to physical suffering, which makes them highly suitable for violent gangs.

A third – important – point that applies to all the cases examined in this chapter is that none is a unified organisation; even if we focus on single groupings, such as the Sinaloa drug cartel in Mexico, it transpires that they are often what have been described as "confederacies". Indeed, one of the striking features of many OC organisations is how much internecine conflict there is. Thus gang warfare within "the bikers" (as in Waco, Texas, in May 2015) or the Russian mafiya (both the thieves-in-law and the 1990s new gangs) has been all too common. Unfortunately, while some might argue that such warfare is a good thing, since the fatalities that are frequently involved mean a reduction in the number of gangsters, all too often innocent members of the public are killed or injured too as "collateral damage".

Fourth, many of the more traditional, hierarchically-organised OC syndicates are in decline. This point was made in the discussion of the Yakuza and the Russian "thieves-in-law", while Chin (2014: 220) notes that only 14 out of an earlier 50 Triad societies are still active. However, this potentially encouraging fact does not appear to apply at present to OMCGs or Mexican drug cartels.

Contrary to popular understanding, it appears that there is in many cases relatively little connection nowadays between the original crime syndicates and diaspora criminal groupings. Thus the links between the Sicilian Mafia and the US-based LCN, or between Chinese OC and ethnically Chinese OC groups in the US, are limited. Increasingly, it is interest in a common product such as drugs, rather than ethnicities, that links groupings in different parts of the world.

An interesting point to emerge from comparative analysis is that totalitarian systems appear to be highly effective at reducing OC; this has been demonstrated here in the case of the Italian Fascists, Mao's China, fascist Japan and Stalin's USSR. However, they are clearly not able to destroy OC groups permanently; as systems become more open, so long-established OC syndicates typically soon make a comeback. Moreover, totalitarian systems can be at least as violent as OC gangs, so that the emergence of the former at the temporary expense of the latter may prove to be a case of "out of the frying pan into the fire" for many citizens.

Finally, it should not be assumed too readily that the general public invariably perceives OC negatively. This has been demonstrated and explained in the case of the Yakuza; but surveys have revealed that Guzmán in Mexico, the Sicilian Mafia on occasions in the past and other OC syndicates have sometimes been seen by local populations as Robin Hoods (no pun intended!).

5 Psycho-social and cultural causes

No social phenomenon can be fully explained by any one particular factor, and anyone who claims otherwise is naïve; OC is no exception to this rule. The reasons why someone decides to set up or join an OCG are multiple, and the particular blend and balance of factors vary by time, place and the individual. An holistic approach is thus required, to allow for almost limitless permutations. Nevertheless, we need to identify the individual components that can help us explain the phenomenon, which requires isolating them – even though, in reality, they interact and overlap. In this chapter, the focus is on the individual and his or her interaction with the society in which they live. This approach is based on structuration theory and the notion of reflexive feedback that was developed by the British sociologist and social theorist Anthony Giddens (1984). This is a complex and sophisticated theory; for our purposes, it basically means that social phenomena, including criminality, are the result of the interplay between human will (agency) and social context (structure). While one of these two may dominate at a particular time, the relationship between them is ultimately always interactive.

Not only is the isolation of individual variables an artificial – albeit necessary – part of the process of better understanding, but the classification of some variables (for example, the impact of conflict) is ultimately somewhat arbitrary; what one analyst considers to be a feature primarily of the individual, another will see as a systemic factor. Fortunately, this is not a significant problem, since, in applying and combining variables and theories considered in this and the next chapter to actual situations, how they were classified when isolated becomes irrelevant.

5.1 Psycho-social approaches

Before considering particular psycho-social explanations of OC, we need to understand what this term means. Psychology literally means "study of the mind", and a psychological approach focuses on the individual's mind and behaviour. Sociology, in contrast, focuses on the collectivity of individuals we call society. So a psycho-social approach examines the interaction between the individual and society. For example, we might examine the impact of age and past experience on OCG membership: do young people who join street gangs later join more sophisticated criminal organisations? How does marginalisation and alienation of the individual in and by society appear to impact upon the propensity to engage in criminal behaviour? A number of theories address these and related questions.

5.1.1 Trait theory

Psychologists sometimes research personalities in terms of traits, which are underlying patterns of behaviour and thought; since these can also be called dispositions, this approach is also known as dispositional theory. One of the most fundamental questions relating to individual traits or dispositions is whether we are born with them or acquire them.

One criminologist who has adopted trait theory for explaining why some people become violent criminals is Lonnie Athens. In a 1989 book, he develops his trait theory by reference to a process of "violentisation". This proceeds through four stages: brutalisation (the individual is coerced into committing violent acts by a member of their group); belligerency (the individual now becomes used to committing violent acts); violent performances (committing violent acts on a regular basis builds the individual's self-esteem); and virulency (which includes the criminal wanting to show off, and feeling extremely self-confident). In his first book on this topic, Athens focuses on individuals, so that his approach is predominantly a psychological (as well as criminological) one. In a follow-up study (Athens 1997), Athens adds analysis of the social context in which violentisation occurs, thus producing a classic example of the psycho-social approach. One clear position adopted by Athens is that traits– including a propensity to engage in violent crime – are not inherited (that is, we are not born with them), but are rather a product of experience.

5.1.2 Strain theory

Two of the most influential social scientists of the nineteenth and twentieth centuries, the French sociologist and social theorist Emile

Durkheim and the American sociologist Robert Merton, are considered to have originally triggered the concept of strain theory. In his classic study of suicide, Durkheim (1951, though 1897 in the original French edition) discusses the concept of anomie, according to which some individuals receive too little moral guidance from society and hence engage in anti-social behaviour; such individuals place their own and their group's standards and interests ahead of those of the wider society in which they live. Merton (1938), influenced by Durkheim's theory of anomie, is generally considered to be the originator of relative deprivation theory, which argues that individuals who see themselves as deprived relative to others in society are more likely to engage in socially deviant behaviour.

The concepts of anomie and relative deprivation informed American sociologist and criminologist Robert Agnew's version of strain theory, which has been used to explain various forms of criminality, including OC. For Agnew (1992: esp. 47 and 50–9), three types of strain can encourage individuals to engage in deviant activity:

1. "Strain as the actual or anticipated failure to achieve positively valued goals" (individuals are unable or believe themselves to be unable to achieve targets seen by society as desirable, such as becoming wealthy).
2. "Strain as the actual or anticipated removal of positively valued stimuli from the individual" (individuals lose the positive influences on them that help to prevent them from engaging in anti-social behaviour).
3. "Strain as the actual or anticipated presentation of negatively valued stimuli" (individuals are influenced by what Agnew calls "noxious stimuli").

Basically, this approach focuses on the ways in which an individual's stress or frustration at being unable to achieve through "normal" channels goals that society considers desirable, losing "good" (positive) influences, and coming into contact with bad (negative) influences can all lead that individual to engage in criminal activity.

Elements of this theory can be found in many other approaches. For instance, in their best-selling book *Freakonomics*, Steven Levitt and Stephen Dubner (2005: 89–114) cite Levitt's research into corner drug dealers in Chicago that reveals that many of them earn less than they would working in McDonalds. Since the latter type of employment would not only generate higher income, but also involve neither the risk of being arrested nor a much higher probability of being killed at work, Levitt and Dubner ask why young people would run the risk of prison sentences or worse by dealing drugs. The answer, apparently, is that many of them wish to achieve wealth and status in a situation where this is all but impossible through the "normal" channels, and have prosperous and feared drug barons as their role-models (heroes), rather than less affluent and less feared or respected (depending on one's perspective) managers of fast food restaurants (for a similar argument applied to young Mexicans see Hernández 2013: 3). This analysis clearly resonates well with, in particular, strain types one and three – though we shall see below that it also relates to rational choice theory and the "sucker mentality" approach.

Another popular book with which elements of strain theory resonate is Francis Fukuyama's *The End of History and the Last Man* (1992). In that, Fukuyama argues that each of us seeks respect or recognition, for which he uses the term *thymos*; if we are unable to secure this through socially approved channels, some will seek it through socially disapproved of "in-groups", such as OCGs.

5.1.3   Labelling theory

Many people assume that labelling theory, also known as "social reaction theory", refers to the fact that how we label something affects our perception of it. The classic example is that one person's terrorist is another person's freedom fighter. But this is not usually what criminologists mean by labelling theory. Rather, this approach maintains that if we label someone a deviant or a criminal, they will then see themselves as such, and continue to engage in criminal activity. The roots of the theory can be traced back to the 1930s and the work of Frank Tannenbaum (1938), while Edwin Lemert (1951) developed it further.

But labelling theory is nowadays primarily associated with Howard Becker (1963), who distinguishes between rule-breakers ("outsiders"), rule-abiders (the law-abiding majority), and rule-makers (basically, the authorities). According to Becker, if the authorities label someone a "delinquent", "deviant" or "criminal" – clearly all pejorative terms – that person will see themselves in that stigmatised way, and will continue to engage in anti-social behaviour. The theory is often used to argue that crime rates increase if we label people criminals too readily (for example, for minor misdemeanours by adolescents), since we have treated someone as an outsider or deviant when it would have been more constructive for both that individual and the public to attempt to integrate them better into mainstream society. Some later versions of labelling theory have placed less emphasis on the role of the authorities' labelling, and more on that of family and friends; if they treat someone as a criminal who is in fact guilty of relatively minor misconduct, that person is more likely to develop into a repeat offender (a.k.a. a recidivist).

5.1.4 Opportunity theory

At the beginning of the 1960s, Richard Cloward and Lloyd Ohlin (1960) published a study in which they argued that a primary factor explaining why individuals did or did not engage in crime, including OC, was opportunity. They identified a number of factors that explained how opportunities differed, including time (usually, committing crime late at night is less likely to be witnessed, making this time more attractive to calculating criminals), place (urban areas are more prone to crime than rural ones), the likelihood of being detected, and the likelihood of avoiding prosecution if caught. While this theory might appear to be an obvious one, the analysis of the different types of opportunity is valuable.

5.1.5 Rational choice theory

In a sense, rational choice theory (RCT) is closely related to opportunity theory, in that it focuses on the choices an individual makes on the basis of perceived costs and benefits. This approach is based on the assumption that individuals (and *arguably* groups – RCT theorists disagree about this) make decisions (choices) on the basis of utility or interest maximisation. In this, it is heavily influenced by mainstream economic theory, while its focus on the individual renders it a liberal (political) theory. If an individual considers engaging in criminal activity, and bases their decision on a (possibly subconscious) analysis of, on the one hand, the likelihood of being detected or of receiving a stiff penalty if prosecuted and convicted, and on the other hand, the likely gain from the criminal act, then their decision is based on a rational choice.

A number of assumptions are common to most versions of RCT. Among them is the concept of consistency (individuals, and perhaps groups, base their decisions on a consistent set of criteria); that preferences are rank-ordered, though two may be equally ranked; and that choices are transitive (in other words, if A is preferred to B, and B to C, then A must be preferred to C). The choice is only *rational* if it is perceived to be utility maximising (that is, the expected payoff is the highest among the various options).

In criminological theory, two of the major proponents of RCT are Derek Cornish and Ronald Clarke (for example, 1986a; 1987); the title of their 1986 edited collection, *The Reasoning Criminal*, encapsulates well their approach. Their basic assumptions are intuitively sensible – that criminals seek through their actions to benefit themselves, and that they make decisions designed to maximise these benefits. Cornish and Clarke acknowledge that the information available to criminals is often imperfect, and that some criminal acts, while being committed impulsively, still involve an element of reasoning; since we are here considering only *organised* crime, the questionability of the latter assumption need not detain us. On the other hand, they distinguish between involvement decisions and event (or criminal act) decisions, and sensibly argue that the rational decision-making process is different in both; the former are relevant in attempting better to understand why people join criminal organisations.

Although their original work focused on RCT applied to burglary, Cornish and Clarke (1986b: 6) do argue that "the rational choice perspective is intended to provide a framework for understanding all forms of crime". One of the important contributions of Cornish and Clarke's RCT approach is that there is a dynamic to it; they maintain that most criminals learn from experience, and therefore typically make more calculated decisions over time. One other point of value to us in Cornish and Clarke's RCT approach is their interest in "displacement". Here, this refers to the reasons why criminals change their targets as opportunities change – be it their victims, the locations in which they operate, or the type of criminal activity in which they engage.

RCT has been heavily criticised from a number of perspectives, including the fact that it assumes we always make decisions on the basis of reason. What if we do things for emotional reasons, such as committing a crime on the spur of the moment without thinking of the consequences? If it seems that this part of the critique cannot apply to *organised* crime, then we need to bear in mind the following. First, we are interested in the motivations of individual members of OCGs as well as of the groups themselves. Second, OCGs sometimes engage in what appears to outsiders to be irrational behaviour, such as risking their lives – losing *everything* – by engaging in turf wars with other groups, when a more rational approach might be to negotiate a compromise, thus only losing *something*. Another criticism that has been raised is that decisions are often made on inadequate or incorrect information, or under severe time constraints, and might in hindsight appear to have been "irrational". Partly to address this general problem of what might look like irrational behaviour, some RCT analysts have devised the concept of bounded rationality, meaning that reason works in conjunction with, and subject to the constraint of, other factors. The problem with this is that it then undermines the fundamental assumptions of RCT.

This is not the place to elaborate the many other drawbacks of RCT (for two of the best critiques see Green and Shapiro 1994; Ariely 2008). But let us assume for the moment that RCT *can* usefully be used to explain *certain forms* of criminality. For example, Ronald Rogowski and Lois Wasserspring (1971; 20–1 – cited in Mason and Galbreath 2004: 558) claim to have identified the rational conditions under which an individual would engage in ethnically-based collective action; since many crime gangs in the past – and some still today – are based on ethnicity, it is worth considering these conditions. Thus, for a rational individual to join a group, Rogowski and Wasserspring argue that the following criteria must be met:

- s/he must be a member of a stigmatised group;
- s/he must perceive some group-specific collective good as desirable;
- ethnic collective action must offer a "cheaper" way of obtaining the good than does (individual) conversion out of the group; and
- s/he must believe that his/her contribution will matter at all in terms of obtaining the desired good.

According to Rogowski and Wasserspring, unless these conditions are met, the individual will not waste time and effort on behalf of the ethnic group.

For some social scientists – though not for Cornish and Clarke, whose approach is nuanced and sensible – RCT is the single most useful theory of human behaviour, indeed the *only* valid theory (for a valuable critique of this position see Lichbach 2003). Such a position is both arrogant and naïve. RCT has much to offer, but our decisions, including whether or not to engage in criminal acts and organisations, are often complex, and can be based on factors other than simple cost–benefit analysis or utility maximisation – unless the latter is interpreted so broadly that it becomes banal and essentially explains nothing.

5.1.6   Sucker mentality

One of the simplest but most insightful explanations of why people join a criminal group, and one which is closely connected to RCT, is described by James Finckenauer and Elin Waring (1998b: 37; see too Finckenauer 2007: 76–8) as the "sucker mentality" syndrome. For these analysts, joining a crime gang can provide a sense of excitement and adventure – despite or because of the risks involved – to the lives of people whose existences would otherwise be rather routine and dull; one would be a sucker to opt for the latter rather than the former. Moreover, many criminals see those who adhere to society's rules as suckers, and that it is therefore legitimate to take advantage of them. For Finckenauer and Waring, such an overall attitude can be seen as a form of RCT. This approach also resonates with the point made by Levitt and Dubner about drug dealers noted above.

5.1.7   Control theory

An insightful and somewhat lateral approach to criminality is control theory. Instead of asking why people become criminals, such as join-ing OC gangs, control theorists turn the question on its head and ask why, if crime can be so rewarding and penalties often so light, most people do *not* become criminals. The theory is associated primarily with Travis Hirschi, who argued in a 1969 book that the answer to this question lies in the notion of the control of the individual not by the state but by the group to which the individual belongs. The strength of the bonds to the group is a crucial determinant of the likelihood of the individual engaging in anti-social behaviour; the weaker they are, the more likely it is that the individual will pursue his or her private (anti-social) interests. Of course, whether or not the group acts as a positive (here meaning encouraging law-abidance) control depends on whether it itself basically respects the law; the assumption is that most groups do.

In a 1990 book, Hirschi teamed up with Michael Gottfredson to produce an updated version of control theory. The book was rather audaciously entitled *A General Theory of Crime*, and the authors really did claim to have a theory that explained all forms of criminality. In this version of the argument, the individual's own self-control is also seen as an important factor; people with limited amounts of self-control are more prone to deviate off the straight and narrow. But self-control is partly a reflection of socialisation processes, so that the individual's relationship with his or her group is also a crucial determinant of their behaviour.

5.1.8   Other psycho-social factors

As demonstrated elsewhere in this book, post-communist states figure prominently among the home bases of TOC. A psycho-social variable that can help us better to understand the turn to OC is the individual's response to a national identity crisis. Whereas most citizens in most post-communist states were relieved to move on from Communist power and what they perceived to be Soviet or specifically Russian domination, many Russians were deeply disappointed by the disinte-gration of the USSR in December 1991 and of the "socialist fraternity of nations", the latter symbolised by the collapse of the Soviet-dominated economic bloc Comecon earlier that year. In a very short period of time (1989–91), Russia lost what is sometimes called the "Outer Empire" (mainly formerly Communist states in Eastern Europe), the "Inner Empire" (that is, the fourteen other republics that, together with Russia itself, constituted the Soviet Union), its role as the home of an alternative to capitalist liberal democracy, its role as the centre of one of the world's (then) two superpowers, and the Cold War. As if this was not enough, many Russians felt humiliated by the crude triumphal-ism of Western commentators such as Francis Fukuyama and then, as the 1990s progressed, by the antics of their own frequently inebriated president, Boris Yeltsin. This sense of humiliation not only explains why so many Russians have supported their assertive, nationalistic but essentially undemocratic leader, Vladimir Putin, in the 2000s, but also why some reacted by turning to feared, violent OC; the line separating fear and respect can be a fine one.

Another factor is the impact of conflict (war) on OC. Some people, mostly men, feel lost in the aftermath of a conflict, and miss the com-radeship they had previously enjoyed with other soldiers. Some also miss what to them was the excitement of battle, and feel that society does not adequately appreciate the sacrifices they made during the conflict. These various aspects of post-conflict reaction can help to explain why so many OC gangs in many parts of the world contain war veterans.

5.1.9   A sceptical approach

The approaches identified so far are sophisticated social science interpretations of why individuals do or do not engage in criminal activity, including OC. But there are also analysts that adopt a much more basic explanation, namely that some people are just inherently evil. For example, Stephen Fox (1989: 76 – cited in Finckenauer 2007: 67), writing about crime in the US, concluded that:

> [OC] derived less from social conditions or difficult childhoods or there-but-for-fortune bad luck than from a durable human condition: the dark, strong pull of *selfish, greedy, impatient, unscrupulous ambition*. (emphasis added)

This simplistic explanation might have some truth to it; the problem, however, is that, in our neo-liberal age of the "me-generation", the pull he describes applies to many – perhaps most – people.

5.2   Cultural explanations

In analysing cultural explanations of OC, we first need to define culture. According to the late Raymond Williams (1976: 76–82 and elsewhere), the term culture is "one of the two or three most complicated words in the English language". He assigns it four principal meanings:

1. Tending or cultivation of something – animals, cereals, etc. (as in agriculture, viticulture).
2. "A general process of intellectual, spiritual and aesthetic development" (used like this since the eighteenth century) – essentially, becoming civilised or cultured.
3. "A particular way of life."
4. "The works and practices of intellectual and especially artistic activity."

For our purposes, the second and third interpretations are the most relevant.

In terms of the component parts of a given culture, we need to ana-lyse the attitudes (views on aspects of the system), beliefs and values (which are deeper, and generally more durable and less malleable than attitudes), and knowledge. Social scientists often assess these in a given culture by examining affective (basically, emotional), evaluative and cognitive (relating to perceptions and knowledge) components. But, while many – though by no means all – societies have a domi-nant set of attitudes and values, there are always minority cultures. These often relate to ethnicity or religion, though there are sometimes also discernible differences between the dominant beliefs and views of city-dwellers and the rural population, young and old, and so on; these various minority views can be called subcultures. But if we are to understand why people join gangs – street gangs to start with, and then sometimes moving on to OC syndicates – it is important to note that there can also be micro-cultures, such as the suburb of a city or even a particular housing estate. The values and attitudes in these micro-cultures can be deeply at odds with those of the larger society, and may be particularly conducive to the development of a criminal mentality.

5.2.1 Class

In terms of subcultures, it is sometimes argued that class position is one of the factors explaining involvement (or not) in criminal activ-ity. Thus Walter Miller (1958), focusing on street gangs, argues that gang behaviour is a crime of what he calls the "lower" classes. But a number of criminologists (for example, Ruggiero 1996; van Duyne, von Lampe and Passas 2002) have noted the class bias of labels such as "underworld" and "upperworld", and the fact that criminals in the latter group, such as white-collar criminals, typically receive far more lenient punishments in most jurisdictions, relative to the impact of their crimes, than criminals in the former group.

5.2.2 Gender

Another cultural argument relates to gender (that is, the social con-struction and socialisation of male and female roles). This argument holds that males and females tend to have different attitudes towards crime and violence. While it is empirically the case that far more men than women engage in OC activity, recent data on convictions of human traffickers from many countries suggest that caution needs to be exercised in making assumptions about the correlation between gender and criminality. Moreover, whereas many traditional OCGs are very macho and patriarchal, and do not normally permit female members, the newer, more loosely organised groupings tend to be much less rigid concerning their members' gender. There were always exceptions even in many of the traditionally male-dominated organisations anyway; recent examples of leading OC women include Giuseppa Vitale of the Sicilian Mafia, Erminia Giuliano of the Naples-based Camorra, Maria Serraino of the Calabria-based 'Ndrangheta, and Xie Caiping of the Triads (nicknamed the "Godmother of Chongqing"). Although there is little evidence of women being actual members (as distinct from wives and lovers) of the Yakuza nowadays, there have been examples in the past.

5.2.3 Ethnicity and cultural conflict theory

A third argument relating to subcultures focuses on ethnicity. One aspect of this focus has resulted in so-called cultural conflict theory. This theory is associated originally with Thorsten Sellin, who in a 1938 article that in fact asks more questions than provides answers, suggested that second generation migrants, in particular, can have torn identities that render them more susceptible to anomic behaviour. Thus, whereas first generation migrants – such as Italians to the USA – have themselves chosen to live in and adapt to their new country, but still have their original culture to provide identity if needed, members of the second generation can sometimes feel that they are neither fully integrated into their receiving country's culture nor have their family's original culture as a fall-back either. This sense of not fully belonging to any one culture can be exacerbated if a member of the first migrant generation marries someone from the destination country, so that a second generation person is from a "mixed" marriage. This sense of being torn between two sets of norms and cultures can, according to the cultural conflict argument, render second generation individuals more susceptible to the attraction of gang membership, which may help to provide them with a cultural identity and a fixed – if anti-social – set of norms.

5.2.4 Social capital theory

In line with several other theories considered in this chapter, social capital theory helps to explain the attraction of OC to some individuals. The three best-known exponents of this theory are Pierre Bourdieu (1986), James Coleman (1988) and Robert Putnam (1993). The first two openly acknowledge that social capital – for our purposes, the trust and sense of reciprocity that builds up between individuals and groups, which can be used to achieve collective (social) ends – can be either positive or, as in the case of OC, negative in its implications and effects. Putnam tends to assume social capital is positive. But while that is problematic for us, his identification of two forms of social capital is useful. He calls this "bonding" and "bridging" social capital. The first refers to social capital that can build up between members of a group, such as an ethnic one; it is something that develops *within* a group. In contrast, bridging capital refers to the trust and reciprocity that can develop *between* groups.

In his original major analysis of social capital, Putnam (1993) argues that Northern Italy functions better than Southern Italy because of its more developed (positive) social capital. Since all the major Italian OC groups originate from Southern Italy, this argument is intriguing. Moreover, to the extent that some essentially national or local OC syndicates are, in a globalising world, increasingly cooperating with OCGs from other countries, the notion of transnational negative bridging capital can be used to interpret this phenomenon. Conversely, while empirical research reveals that criminal groups of similar ethnicity but in different countries – such as the Italian Mafia and LCN in the US, or Chinese gangs in different countries – do not collaborate nowadays as much as they once were assumed to have done, in the few cases where such cooperation does occur between those in the home country and diaspora groups, the concept of negative bonding capital can help to explain this.

5.2.5   Other cultural factors that may relate to OC

Many aspects of a society's dominant culture or significant subcultures have been argued to relate to the salience of OC. One is religion. According to some analysts, American (Catholic) Italians have in the past been seen to be more likely to engage in OC than their WASP (white Anglo-Saxon Protestant) neighbours (van Duyne and van Dijck 2007: 103). One of the more interesting explanations proffered for this is that Catholics can offload their sins via the confessional, whereas Protestants have to accept and live with their own guilt. While this argument intuitively appears questionable, it is at least worth consideration in light of van Dijk's (2007: 43) claim noted in Chapter 3 that there is a clear pattern to the distribution of OC in Europe. This observation is of relevance here because the pattern van Dijk identifies correlates with religious cultural traditions; north west Europe mostly has a Protestant tradition, Spain and Italy are both Catholic countries, while the dominant religious tradition in Russia and Ukraine is Orthodox Christianity (in Albania, it is Islam).

However, the limited empirical evidence on the connections between criminality – generally, not specifically relating to OC – and religion is at least mixed, sometimes contradictory. Thus, while one study (Baier and Wright 2001) suggests that religious people are less likely to commit criminal acts, another (Zuckerman 2009) finds that atheists, at least in the USA, tend to engage in serious crime *less* than religious people.

There are at least two reasons why the connection between OC and religion has been largely neglected by empirical researchers. One is that it is assumed that most OCG members are unlikely to have been strongly influenced by the religious culture of their home countries; after all, most religions reject violence, theft, deception and other activities typical of OCGs. The other is that the leading TOC syndicates hail from countries with a wide range of religious traditions anyway – or, in the case of the Triads and other Chinese OCGs, ones with no major religious tradition at all.

It is sometimes claimed that attitudes towards *hierarchy* help to explain differential rates of OC activity, with more hierarchical societies likely to have higher levels of OC activity, particularly of the traditional, highly structured type. Another aspect of this variable relates directly to THB. Thus human trafficking is sometimes argued to be worse from countries with a very patriarchal culture; patriarchy is a gender-based form of hierarchy.

Following on from the previous point is the notion that attitudes towards the state may correlate with OC rates. For instance, a state that enjoys a low level of popular legitimacy is likely to suffer from more OC activity than a more legitimate system. Of course, this can relate to structural factors, which are considered in the next chapter; the low level of legitimacy might in part be because of the ineffectiveness of the state, including its poor provision of law-enforcement. But another dimension of attitudes towards the state is that there is still a tradition in some cultures of citizens resolving problems themselves, often within the context of a clan, rather than turning to the state for assistance. Apparently low rates of OC activity in such states, when this seems to be at odds with popular perception, may thus relate to the fact that crimes are simply not being reported to the police.

5.2.6   Questioning or redefining the cultural approach

According to Martin O'Brien (2005), there is what its proponents see as a current paradigm shift in the study of crime, called "cultural criminology". He cites a definition of this from Keith Hayward and Jock Young (2004: 259):

> the placing of crime and its control in the context of culture; that is, viewing both crime and the agencies of control as cultural products – as creative constructs.

While sensitivity to cultural difference might appear to be a good thing, O'Brien argues forcefully that it has gone too far, and that focusing on subjectivity, such as including emotion in explaining crime, overlooks the fact that criminals in any culture often make decisions based on rational choices. He thus urges caution in going too far down this path, and reveals himself to be more in favour of hard-nosed empirical mainstream approaches, which cultural criminologists themselves often criticise for being "conservative", too quantitative, and too positivistic. O'Brien maintains that much of cultural criminology is confused and contradictory, politically-driven (left-wing, sometimes anarchistic), and fails to make persuasive links between the actions of individual criminals and the cultural context in which they operate. Indeed, he argues, cultural criminologists have not even adequately and clearly defined what they mean by culture. In short, O'Brien's critique of the relatively new cultural approach to criminology reveals that the latter is still far from being generally accepted among criminologists, some of whom see it as merely "trendy", and both less original and less scholarly than its advocates maintain.

5.3   Conclusions

In seeking to use psycho-social approaches to understand why some people engage in OC and most do not, the most important point to determine is whether negative (anti-social) stimuli appear to outweigh positive ones. All of the psycho-social approaches outlined in this chapter – which are mostly compatible with each other and often overlap – can be interpreted and employed in terms of this simple question. One factor that can help us to determine this is the study of a given culture's or subculture's values; engaging in such targeted (that is, culturally sensitive) research renders it more feasible to devise policies designed to reduce OC, including its role in THB, in specific contexts.

However, O'Brien is correct to warn us against excessive emphasis on culture and to remind us of the role of rational agency in the scale and nature of OC in particular countries or even transnationally. For instance, both Singapore and Hong Kong have similar Sinic and Confucian cultures, yet have had very different experiences of OC in recent decades. Perhaps, then, culture (including religious traditions and ethnicity) is usually best seen as an intervening variable – one that moderates a more deep-seated explanatory ("independent") variable, such as poverty, extreme inequality, or the political will of a leadership team.

This leads us to remind the reader of the importance of the introductory caveats: if structuration theory is correct, both individual choice and decisions on the one hand, and structural constraints and opportunities (context) on the other, play a role in determining involvement or not in OC and the trafficker side of THB; trafficking victims have not made the decision to be trafficked, so that it is quite inappropriate to analyse reasons for their situation based on choice. In this chapter, we have focused on the individual's choices and the cultural context; but these must be combined with broad systemic factors if we are to achieve a reasonably full and convincing understanding of the drivers of OC: these factors are the primary focus of the next chapter.

6   System-related causes

It will be recalled from the previous chapter that the analytical approach adopted here is a version of structuration theory, meaning for our purposes that most social phenomena are best explained as the result of the dynamic interaction between human will (agency) and the context in which we operate (structure). It will further be recalled that an holistic approach is needed to explain the scale and nature of OC in particular countries and regions, but that the individual components of such an approach need to be isolated and analysed for the sake of a clearer understanding. Thus, as in Chapter 5, the various factors and theories are artificially separated here; in reality, they overlap and interact.

6.1   "Fortress Europe" in a "borderless world"

In 1990, Kenichi Ohmae published a book with the intriguing title of *The Borderless World*. In this, he argued that the rise of the global consumer meant that the traditional borders between states were being whittled away, and that the role of the state is diminishing. In the era of the Internet, and as more and more consumers purchase goods online from other countries, much of Ohmae's argument is persuasive. But it needs to be remembered that this is first and foremost a management book, and that Ohmae perceives the world primarily from a business perspective. While the world's borders have become ever more permeable for *capital*, goods and services, the plight of refugees and asylum seekers demonstrates clearly that many *people* cannot move across borders nearly so easily.

It is true that human movement within many parts of Europe has become much easier, with the mooting in 1985 and then introduction in 1995 of the Schengen Area, whereby, at least in theory, once in that area of 26 states (22 EU countries plus Iceland, Liechtenstein, Norway and Switzerland; the UK is not a member), a person can move from country to country without being required to present a passport at any frontier. But at the same time as the Schengen Area was being touted as a symbol of greater freedom to travel, critics started referring to Fortress Europe. This was not a new term; it had been coined during the Second World War. But it took on a new – and clearly negative – meaning in the 1990s. In part in response to criticisms, the EU promised in 1999 to standardise asylum and immigration policies within five years. Although much progress has been made in this area (for example, the European Pact on Immigration and Asylum 2008, and the establishment of the European Asylum Support Office in Malta in 2010), there was still no final agreement on asylum at the time of writing.

Some understanding of why critics have referred to Fortress Europe can be gleaned from the following data. In 2002, the EU received some 490,000 applications for asylum; the total success rate for such applications was 20 per cent.[1] The proportion accepted has increased since then, with approximately 110,000 people being granted asylum in 2012 out of a total of some 297,000 (that is, c. 37 per cent), although there are significant differences between member states in terms of acceptance rates. But the 2012 figure more than doubled in 2014, when some 626,000 people applied to the EU for asylum; this said, the highest figure until 2015 was in 1992, when there were 672,000 applications (Eurostat 2015b). It should be clear that people smuggling and human trafficking thrive in such a situation, as desperate people turn to criminal organisations to help them enter Europe illegally. Unfortunately, this has significant potential downsides, in addition to the coercion and violence involved in trafficking. One of the grimmest statistics relating to the asylum-seeking situation is that, as of end-2013, more than 17,000 refugees had died attempting to enter "Fortress Europe" since 1993: the main cause, accounting for nearly 10,000 deaths, was drowning. That figure has since increased, particularly in 2015, as the number of Syrian refugees has escalated.

The reference to Syria leads us to isolate another factor that plays into the hands of TOC, especially gangs involved in people smuggling and THB, namely the impact of conflict. While the number of wars between states has declined in recent decades, the number of civil wars has not. Understandably, many citizens seek to save themselves and their families from the horrors of such wars. But if other countries appear to be at least reluctant – even overtly unwilling, as Hungary has been in 2015 – to admit refugees, the demand for people smuggling increases. While people smuggling and THB are conceptually distinct, in reality the former all too often mutates into the latter; as "people smugglers" claim that the costs (and hence prices) of smuggling have increased, and those being smuggled are unable to meet the higher payments, so the latter are frequently required to pay off their "debts" through forced labour of various kinds.

6.2   Poverty and inequality

It is often argued that a major cause of crime – which can include OC – is deprivation and poverty; according to an old saying, "poverty is the mother of crime". Unfortunately, comprehensive and reliable over time statistics on the percentage of the population living below the poverty line in a given country are not available; the data are patchy. But we can begin our analysis of the possible correlation between socio-economic factors and the salience of OC in a given society by considering some of the available statistics. Thus the percentage of the population living below the poverty line ("poverty headcount ratio at national poverty lines") for our selected countries (see Chapter 3) is as follows, with the year of the assessment in brackets:

- Albania – 25.4 (2002); 14.3 (2012)
- Australia – 13.0 (2010); 13.9 (2012)
- Bulgaria – 21.8 (2008); 21.0 (2013)
- Cambodia – 34.0 (2008); 17.7 (2012)
- Canada – 15.0 (1997); 8.8 (2011)
- China – 4.6 (1998); c. 7.6 (2013)
- Italy – 19.6 (2011)
- Japan – 16.0 (2010)
- Mexico – 47.0 (2005); 52.3 (2012)
- Moldova – 26.3 (2009); 12.7 (2013)
- Nigeria – 48.4 (2003); 46.0 (2009)
- Romania – 23.4 (2007); 22.6 (2011)
- Russia – 13.0 (2009); 11.0 (2013)
- Serbia – 24.6 (2011)
- Thailand – 20.9 (2007); 13.2 (2011)
- United Kingdom – 16.2 (2011)
- United States – 14.5 (2013)

Sources: All except Australia, Canada, China (2013), Italy, Japan UK and USA – http://data.worldbank.org/country/ (accessed 1 March

2015): Australia – Davidson and Evans (2014: 8); Canada – Statistics Canada; China 2013 – State Council; Italy and Japan – Nationmaster; UK – Eurostat; USA – United States Census Bureau.

The above statistics – which, especially given the variety of sources, should not be treated as authoritative – suggest that the correlation between poverty levels and involvement in OC is either weak or complex. Thus, while the Mexican poverty rate might help to explain the attraction of OC to many Mexicans (see Ramsey 2011) or the vulnerability to THB in Nigeria, the fact that the recent poverty levels in Albania and Australia are very similar, while the salience of OC activity in them apparently differs significantly, suggests that other factors must be at play.

Another indication that poverty might be a major problem in a society is the unemployment rate, so it is worth examining this in the countries focused on in this study that appear to have had particularly serious problems with OC and/or THB. While World Bank data 1991–2013 (World Bank 2014) suggest that unemployment might have been a major driver of OC in some countries, notably Albania (annual averaged rate between 16.9 per cent and 22.7 per cent over this period), Bulgaria (5.6 per cent – 21.4 per cent), Serbia (12.6 per cent – 23.9 per cent) and arguably Russia (5.2 per cent – 13.3 per cent), the data on countries such as Cambodia (0.2 per cent – 2.5 per cent), China (3.8 per cent – 4.9 per cent), Mexico (2.5 per cent – 6.9 per cent) and Thailand (0.7 per cent – 3.4 per cent) – assuming they are reasonably accurate, which might be questionable – encourage us to look for further explanations.

But before doing so, since we have opted to focus on THB as a major dimension of contemporary TOC, it is important to note in this discussion of unemployment that the rates often vary quite considerably between men and women. High levels of unemployment or underemployment among women, especially unskilled ones, render them more vulnerable to becoming trafficking victims of OCGs.

Another way of analysing the potential role of poverty is to consider *relative* impoverishment – that is, whether or not poorer citizens are becoming poorer not in absolute terms, but relative to others in society. A common method of assessing this is to look at Gini coefficients, which, crudely, measure the income differential between rich and poor. Gini coefficients are usually scaled 0–100, where 0 represents total equality of income distribution, and 100 perfect inequality. Most analysts agree that a Gini coefficient below 30 indicates that a society is relatively egalitarian; scores of 30–40 represent a medium level of income inequality; while scores above 40 indicate that a society is very unequal. Let us now consider the Gini coefficients of the countries selected for particular consideration.

Unfortunately, it is not possible to provide directly comparable Gini coefficient data, since the most commonly used sources cite different years and are not up-to-date. With these caveats in mind, comparing World Bank data from the mid-2000s (World Bank 2015) suggests that Serbia and Bulgaria have had relatively low Gini coefficients (below 30) in recent years, while Cambodia, China, Mexico, Nigeria (UN data), Russia, Thailand and the USA have had high rates (over 40) – with the remaining eight countries all having medium levels. Although high levels of OC correlate with a high Gini coefficient (48.5 in 1995, 48.2 in 2008) in Mexico, no clear overall cross-country pattern emerges from the data; the Gini coefficient does not correlate strongly with perceived OC, and only slightly better with THB source countries.

6.3   Corruption

Although the connections between corruption and OC are increasingly being recognised, this is a recent development; for too long, corruption was overlooked as a factor explaining the scale and nature of (T)OC. Yet collusion between corrupt officials and OCGs has long been a major security and crime problem. Among the most common areas of such collusion nowadays are drug trafficking, people smuggling, THB, illegal prostitution, arms trafficking and illegal gambling. The state officers most frequently involved in these are immigration and customs officials, border guards, and police officers – although local council officials can also be involved (for instance, in illegally supplying local residence and work permits), as can politicians. Regarding the last of these, it was pointed out in Chapter 1 that a key distinction drawn between OC generally and mafias is that the latter directly interact with political actors, whereas other OCGs usually avoid the authorities as much as possible.

The ways in which corrupt officers of the state collude with OC vary. A common scenario is where officers at border crossings turn a blind eye to gangs smuggling goods (for example, drugs, cigarettes, oil) across the frontier in return for a bribe. Again in return for a bribe (for example, cash, drugs, free sexual services), police officers sometimes tip off illegal brothels in which there are THB victims about an impending raid, giving those running the brothel time to hide their victims.

Analysts of corruption often distinguish between petty (or low-level) and grand (a.k.a. high-level or elite) corruption. Most of the cases cited in the previous paragraph constitute examples of the former; but high-level collusion, such as between government ministers and OC syndicates, is often more serious in terms of its overall impact on society. Unfortunately, measuring it is even more difficult than measuring petty corruption. For instance, we can and do survey citizens about whether or not they have paid a bribe in the previous 12 months, and can use the results to suggest that country A is more corrupt than country B. But since most citizens do not come into contact with high-level officials, our data on popular experience of bribery tells us almost nothing about high-level corruption.

Partly because of this problem, most analysts continue to place more faith in perception indices, of which the most frequently cited is Transparency International's annual (since 1995) Corruption Perceptions Index (CPI). The data in the CPIs must be treated with caution for various reasons (see Galtung 2006: esp. 106–25; but see too Saisana and Saltelli 2012). Nevertheless, in the absence of anything better, they provide some idea of how people see the world, or at least particular countries (for all CPIs since 1995 see Transparency International 2015). This is important, since perception is a form of reality; we make all sorts of decisions – such as whether or not to invest in a country, or to sell our shares – on perceptions. Assuming that the CPI perceptions scores do bear some resemblance to the "real" situation in individual countries, it is noteworthy that many states particularly associated with TOC are also perceived to have had relatively high levels of corruption since the 1990s. This point does not hold in all cases, however; Japan, home of the Yakuza, appears to have had relatively low levels of corruption. But this is probably the exception that proves the rule: while correlation does not prove causality, common sense tells us that high levels of OC activity are usually in part a function of high levels of corruption.

6.4   Weak state theory

While this factor has not featured prominently in most analyses, one of the key drivers of OC and THB in some countries is weak states. In political science, still the most frequently cited definition of the state is that provided by the German social scientist Max Weber in the early twentieth century. For him (in *Politics as a Vocation*, 1919 – in Gerth and Wright Mills 1970: 78), the state is "a human community that (successfully) claims the *monopoly of the legitimate use of physical force* within a given territory" (emphasis in original). So what is a *weak* state? In a nutshell, it is one that does not meet Weber's criterion of successfully upholding a claim to "the monopoly of the legitimate use of physical force" within its territory and poorly serves its citizens.

One analyst who has applied weak state theory to post-communist transition states is Venelin Ganev (2001). He cites Kazimierz Poznanski (1992: 211), who argues that "The disintegration of Communism has meant inevitable weakening of the state." This is because Communist parties in essence ran the state; with the collapse of Communism, many former Communists had a vested interest in exploiting rather than strengthening the new state. This takes us a little way along the path of a weak state theory of OC; but Ganev does not explore this issue, and we need to find our own way.

First, we need a more detailed picture of what constitutes a weak state, and how this relates to OC. A useful starting point is Stewart Patrick's analysis (2006: 27) of "the world's most poorly governed countries", which he defines as follows:

> Poorly performing developing countries are linked to humanitarian catastrophes; mass migration; environmental degradation; regional instability; global pandemics; international crime; the proliferation of weapons of mass destruction (WMD); and, of course, transnational terrorism.

This definition explicitly identifies TOC ("international crime") as a feature of what can be called weak states, and parts of his article (esp. 38–40) explore the relationship between such states and OC. Patrick argues persuasively that the relationship between TOC and weak states is a complex one. For instance, weak states are almost always impoverished; TOC is profit-oriented, and while it might originate in weak states, it is likely to target and operate in more affluent and functional states. Another sensible point made by Patrick is that not all weak or fragile states are the same, and the type of OC that might be partly explained by weakness in one of the four main areas of governance he argues should be examined in assessing a given country (physical security; legitimate political institutions; economic management; and social welfare – Patrick 2006: 29–30, 40) may not be replicated in what appears to be a similar second country.

Between 2005 and 2013, the US-based Fund for Peace produced an annual "Failed States Index"; wisely, this has been re-named the "Fragile States Index" (FSI) since 2014. This index assesses how effective individual states are by producing a score out of ten for 12 variables; the higher the score, the less effective the state on that variable (Fund for Peace 2015), so that the worst possible score is 120.

Now that the Failed States Index has been re-named the Fragile States Index, the borderline between states with varying degrees of serious problems has become even more blurred. However, the FSI itself provides different classifications for more and less troubled states. Using this, we can call the 38 most troubled states (those the FSI classifies as "Very High Alert", "High Alert" and "Alert") in the 2015 FSI "fragile", and the next two groups ("High Warning" and "Warning"), comprising 69 states, as merely "weak". Using this somewhat arbitrary approach, it emerges that none of the countries identified in this study as the home base of a major TOC grouping is classified as fragile,[2] while four are weak (Russia, China, Serbia, Mexico). But since many countries in which TOC is based are classified as neither fragile nor weak, the most we can say is that weak state theory is limited in its ability to explain TOC.

6.5   Post-communism

Since several of the states on which we are concentrating are post-communist, it is worth examining aspects of post-communism that appear to increase the likelihood of both OC and THB (on post-communism generally see Holmes 1997). Some of these variables have already been considered, including unemployment and Gini coefficients. But others are peculiar to post-communist transition states, and should be considered in their own right.

During the Communist era, the state owned most property, yet claimed that the systems were "workers' states" and "people's democracies". Since there were often shortages of basic goods, many citizens therefore had no qualms about stealing from their workplace; after all, in theory all property belonged to the people. With the emergence of post-communism and privatisation, it became much more difficult to steal from work; given the uncertainties and insecurity of early post-communism, however, many citizens became desperate, thus rendering them more susceptible to temptation (in the case of criminals) or vulnerable (in the case of trafficked persons).

This situation was compounded by several other factors. One was that most post-communist states initially had little in the way of a welfare system. During the Communist era, welfare had largely been administered by the workplace; with the collapse of the old system, this arrangement rapidly disappeared. Moreover, most Communist systems had strongly discouraged religion (Albania was the only Communist state actually to ban religion), claiming that morality should be inculcated by the state, which was to develop the "new socialist person". With the collapse of Communism, this value system rapidly disappeared too; while some citizens now enjoyed the freedom to pursue their religious beliefs openly, others had been subjected for so long to an atheistic ideology that they found it difficult to turn to religion. In short, there was a moral vacuum, which is conducive to higher crime rates.

A problem of transition states generally, but which has been far more acute in post-communist states, is legislative lag. Whereas many countries in Latin America, Southern Europe, Africa and Asia have experienced political transitions in recent decades, most of these did not have to undergo the multiple transitions former Communist states have; in addition to political change, the latter have undergone significant changes in the economy (marketisation and privatisation), social structure (creating a bourgeoisie), social welfare, education, law, and international allegiances. This placed a severe strain on lawmakers, who needed to adopt brand new laws across a vast array of policy areas. The problem was compounded by the fact that there had been no tradition of political compromise or a loyal opposition in the Communist era, and changing an entrenched decision-making culture takes time; political squabbling often led to the policymaking process in early post-communism being far more protracted than it should have been. Finally, many politicians were corrupt, and had a vested interest in delaying or blocking the adoption of laws that would render it more difficult for them to exploit the situation. The relevance of this to OC is that laws that could and should have prevented or hindered OC were in many cases not passed for years, or else were severely – and often deliberately – flawed.

This leads to another aspect of post-communism, although it can be found in other kinds of system, namely "state capture". This was briefly mentioned in Chapter 2, but can be explored in further detail here. At the start of this century, the World Bank began to promote this concept with particular reference to post-communist transition states, and defined it as follows:

> the capacity of firms to *shape and affect the formation* of the basic rules of the game (i.e., laws, regulations and decrees) through private payments to public officials and politicians. (Hellman, Jones and Kaufmann 2000: iv, original emphasis)

and

> failure of the state to provide certain basic public goods (such as security, land title, a legal system to provide orderly dispute resolution) may cause certain business groups to capture the state to provide protection for their business investments but not those of others. (World Bank 2009)

This is an insightful approach, but needs to be broadened, so that the term "business groups" explicitly includes OCGs. After all, many academics and government authorities nowadays classify OC as a form of enterprise.

One of the few positive aspects of Communist systems was that many of them provided world class scientific-technical education and training. Unfortunately, this expertise has sometimes been put to criminal use since the 1990s, with Russians and Ukrainians featuring strongly among cybercriminals (Glenny 2011; Holmes 2015a), while Romanians and Bulgarians have often been implicated in sophisticated forms of ATM skimming.

A salient, and to some surprising, aspect of the collapse of Communism was that it was for the most part relatively peaceful. In most countries, rather than violently defend the old Communist system, the Communist elites preferred to "go with the flow" and secure for themselves a front row privileged seat in the new post-communist system.

But the break-up of Yugoslavia in the 1990s was an exception; there, the transition to a new arrangement was protracted and bloody. In Communist times, Serbia had been the most populous and dominant republic, despite various efforts over the years at making the republics more equal. As one republic after another broke away from former Yugoslavia, with Slovenia and Croatia leading the way, many Serbs became increasingly resentful, and engaged in open warfare with their former comrades. The worst case was in Bosnia and Herzegovina. Much of the Western world heavily criticised Serbia for its actions, and imposed sanctions. But this had unintended consequences. In response to the sanctions, the Serbian government either turned a blind eye or else actively encouraged – this is not clear – OC to smuggle in goods that had become difficult to obtain because of the West's actions. Once the conflicts were over, some Serbs preferred to continue with their illegal means of generating income. This point about sanctions-busting and post-conflict situations applies to many other states, not merely post-communist ones.

A final feature of post-communism to note is that it became much easier in the 1990s for citizens of former Communist states to travel to other countries. During the Communist era, most citizens found it very difficult to secure permission from their own authorities to travel abroad, other than to other Communist states. This new free-dom under post-communism was soon exploited by OCGs, especially as the West became less welcoming following the short-lived euphoria at the very beginning of the 1990s about the collapse of Communism.

6.6   Institutionalisation

The previous two factors analysed focused on state deficiencies that appear to correlate with an increased incidence of OC and THB. But another way of looking at this is to focus on institutional arrangements that appear to *reduce* the relative scale of these activities. In general, for instance, robust democracies have fewer problems with OC than do other types of system. A well-entrenched rule of law culture, which typically goes hand in glove with a robust democracy, normally has less OC than cultures in which there is less respect for the law. Van Dijk (2007: 46) takes this point one step further, maintaining that his findings for the COCI (see Chapter 3) support the argument made by others that the single best predictor of the scale of OC activity in a given jurisdiction is the level of the judiciary's independence: the higher this is, the lower the incidence of OC.

6.7 Globalisation

One of the most common explanations nowadays for the apparent marked rise of OC in recent years, especially TOC, is globalisation (for example, Albanese and Reichel 2014; see too Hall 2013). Unfortunately, there are still significant differences on the precise meaning of this term and what it covers (for useful introductions see Stiglitz 2002; Steger 2013). However, there is a solid core, about which there is almost universal agreement. The first point to note is the second part of the word, "-isation"; this makes it clear that the term refers to a process or dynamic. The process is generally seen to be towards a *telos* or end goal, namely globality. In the early-1960s, Canadian philosopher Marshall McLuhan revealed extraordinary prescience when he identified a coming communications technology revolution that would turn the world increasingly into what he called a "global village" (McLuhan 1962, 1964). For many, globalisation is primarily about this communications revolution, which has dramatically increased interconnectedness between people and organisations. For others, however, it is the economic dimension of globalisation that is its defining characteristic.

Quite when globalisation emerged is highly contested. However, the most common view is that globalisation has emerged since the late-1980s as a result of the spread of neo-liberalism, the development of the Internet, and the ramifications of the collapse of Communism. Globalisation has many aspects, the economic and communications-related being only two of them. In addition, there are social, cultural, environmental, political and legal, and ideological dimensions. Each is examined briefly here and related to OC.

6.7.1 Economic

In addition to the implications of the so-called borderless world and Fortress Europe (or, we can add, Fortress USA, Fortress Australia, and so on) for OC and THB, other economic aspects of globalisation can help us better to understand the increasing transnationalism of many OC syndicates. One of these has been noted by Manuel Castells (2010: 174), who adopts what is essentially a version of enterprise theory (see below) combined with the globalisation-related *pax mafiosa* thesis.

Among other things, Castells discusses the ease of money laundering in the contemporary world, which is another driver of the internationalisation of OC. In 2013, the Tax Justice Network (TJN, established 2009) produced a Financial Secrecy Index (FSI) that provides insight into how easy it is to launder money. One way of assessing this is by measuring the willingness of states to allow their banks to operate in a largely secretive manner, which plays into the hands of money launderers. Using this criterion, the world's worst offenders are mostly tiny (population-wise) island states; in order (worst first), they are Samoa, Vanuatu, the Seychelles, St. Lucia and Brunei Darussalam. However, the TJN itself prefers to criticise most strongly not these tiny states, but rather those that play the greatest role in international money laundering; again in order, starting with the worst, these are Switzerland, Luxemburg, Hong Kong, Cayman Islands, Singapore and the USA (all from FSI 2013). This list paints a very different picture from the first of who is most to blame for the ease with which international money laundering is carried out in the contemporary globalised world.

Another well-known analyst of the role of globalisation in OC is Moisés Naím (2003: 29–30), who argues that globalisation not only expands illegal markets, but also imposes heavier economic burdens on governments (for example, they have to tighten public budgets in order to compete with other countries); this can impact negatively on the resources available for law enforcement.

6.7.2   Communications related

In discussing globalisation, analysts have referred to "the death of distance" (Cairncross 1997), or "time and space compression" (Harvey 1990). By this they mean, among other things, that the communications revolution has rendered it much easier than it used to be to communicate with others, no matter how physically or temporally distant they may be. There are four principal ways in which this revolution – symbolised above all by the rise of the Internet since the 1990s – plays into the hands of OC.

First, criminals have been able to use the Net to market their goods and services, including illicit drugs, high interest loans, sex and so on. As one aspect of this, online advertising is now one of the main methods for attracting people, usually via highly misleading job descriptions, who will subsequently become THB victims. Second, cybercriminals use the Net to steal "identities", meaning that they can find individuals' coordinates, including credit card details, which can then be used to steal from those individuals, including from their bank accounts; computer-based identity theft is an increasingly serious problem globally. Third, the Net can be used for money laundering, via hard to trace wire transfers (electronic funds transfers). Finally, clever use of the Net can render criminal organisations more invisible to law enforcement agencies than when they are physically present in a given location, and thus more difficult to track down and prosecute.

6.7.3   Cultural

A common criticism of globalisation is that it has a detrimental effect on cultures and cultural difference. While some argue that globalisation increases tolerance of other cultures, others maintain that its homogenising tendency means that many people consider their cultural distinctiveness – their very identity – to be under threat (Featherstone 1990). While the latter argument is often cited as an explanation for Islamist terrorism, the notion that globalisation can lead to deep alienation may also help to explain the attraction of OC, though this needs to be empirically researched.

6.7.4   Social

A frequently cited advantage of globalisation is that it has brought huge numbers of people, mainly in developing countries, out of poverty. There is no question that economic globalisation has improved the lot of billions of people; China and India, for example – which between them account for more than a third of the world's population – have been experiencing impressive economic growth in recent years largely as a result of globalisation, which in turn has led to a significant improvement in the living standards of hundreds of millions of people in those countries. One ramification of this is that there is now a much larger market – a bigger middle class – than there was a quarter of a century ago for all sorts of goods and services, including those typically provided by OC.

While globalisation has improved the lot of millions in the developing world, it has also had a negative impact on some in developed countries. Unskilled and semi-skilled workers, in particular, have often found that their jobs have been outsourced overseas, leaving them unemployed. For some, this renders the temptation to engage in profitable but illegal activity that much greater; while most resist this temptation, others do not.

6.7.5 Environmental

The Chernobyl nuclear disaster of 1986 made it abundantly clear that many environmental problems cannot be contained within the borders of individual sovereign states, and numerous measures have been adopted by governments to address these. Unfortunately, increasingly strict environmental regulations in many parts of the world can encourage (T)OC activity. Crime gangs are not generally concerned about environmental damage, and sometimes sponsor illegal tree-felling in developing countries, for example, so as to be able to sell timber in developed countries at a much lower price than is charged for legally harvested timber.

OC has also played a significant role in hazardous waste disposal, both domestic and transnational (Block and Scarpitti 1985). Since many states find it increasingly difficult to dispose of toxic waste in a manner that is both environmentally friendly and acceptable to the public, (T)OC has taken advantage of this problem, and sometimes dumps materials that constitute serious health risks (see Chapter 2).

6.7.6 Political and legal

While states increasingly recognise that their economies are part of a much larger entity – the global market – most still jealously guard their political and legal sovereignty, nowadays in part precisely as a reaction to globalisation. This emphasis on sovereignty can play into the hands of OCGs. An obvious example is that some states find it difficult to conclude extradition treaties with other states, partly because of differences in legal systems and unwillingness to compromise on these; this is clearly advantageous to TOC.

6.7.7 Ideological

The ideology most associated with globalisation is neo-liberalism (for an excellent introduction see Harvey 2005). Several dimensions of neo-liberalism can be conducive to the rise of OC. These include the notions that ends (results) are more important than means (proper process); that the state should deregulate as much as possible, which can send the message that it is abjuring its responsibilities to protect citizens; and that long and loyal service by their officers counts for little when states decide to downsize, outsource and privatise.

6.7.8   Glocalisation

Before concluding this analysis of the ways in which globalisation can contribute to the rise of TOC, it needs to be acknowledged that some analysts argue that the discourse on TOC has been distorted, in that it exaggerates the phenomenon's scale, largely for political reasons. Thus Dick Hobbs (1998: 407) refers to "the political science inspired moral panics that have emerged as a response to the fragmentation of the Eastern bloc and found a home within the budget wars of declining western states". He goes on to argue that OC is in reality far more localised than the TOC discourse acknowledges. This is a valuable corrective, or at least an argument to make us stop and think. Ultimately, however, *both* local and transnational OC are serious concerns and *both* need to be addressed, whatever their respective scales.

6.8   Enterprise theory

An increasingly popular interpretation of OC is that it is simply a particular form of enterprise. This argument has been made notably by Dwight C. Smith (1975, 335–47; 1980) and R. Thomas Naylor (1997, 2002), and has been adopted by, for example, the UK authorities. According to Smith, enterprise should be considered along a spectrum, from legal business through white-collar crime to OC. Displaying a penchant for alliteration, he describes this spectrum as running from paragons through pariahs to pirates, and provides concrete examples, such as the spectrum from legitimate banking to loan sharking. Among the similarities he sees between licit corporations and criminal organisations is that many of the latter are also professionally managed, hierarchically structured, market based and profit-oriented.

Enterprise theorists often make the point that illicit enterprises typically provide goods and services that are either not provided by licit enterprises because they are illegal (for example, many kinds of drugs; products from endangered species) or in short supply, or else are much more expensive in the legal market – to no small extent because the legal provider has directly or indirectly paid all the costs, such as wages and taxes, whereas OC may well have stolen the goods and not paid anything other than transportation and distribution costs.

A recent example of this that potentially affects many consumers, and is an area most would not associate with OC, is the marked increase in counterfeit olive oil that was reported in the British media in 2015 (for example, Bawden 2015). Italy is one of the world's leading producers of olive oil, but a poor harvest resulting from bad weather and the spread of disease in the olive groves in 2014–15 led to a substantial price rise. As a result, OC moved much more energetically than in the past (it has been involved in deceptive marketing of olive oil for years) into the production of impure oil, which it marketed as high quality olive oil. In this way, it was able to take advantage of both the higher prices the genuine oil was commanding and the unmet demand.

Recalling a point made in Chapter 1, a final aspect for comparison is that both legal and illegal enterprises often seek to create a monopoly, which can result in turf wars. But whereas legal enterprises are usually restrained in their efforts by anti-trust (a.k.a. known as anti-monopoly or trade practices) laws, there are no such constraints on criminal organisations. Moreover, while both corporations and criminal organisations often seek to collude with other organisations to create an oligopoly, or what might be called a group monopoly, legal enterprises are limited in this by anti-cartel laws, whereas OC gangs are not.

The enterprise model assumes various forms in analyses of OC. One of the better known ones is supply chain theory. This has mostly been applied in studies of drug trafficking, and emphasises the different stages – links in a chain – of the process, from manufacture through transportation to retail selling (Wright 2006: 89–92). Once again, the similarities with the way in which legal enterprise operates should be obvious.

Louise Shelley (2003: 123–30) has produced a nuanced "business model" approach specifically to THB, in which she identifies six distinct versions:

1. The natural resource model – typical of post-Soviet OC
   This model is short-term; affects "almost exclusively" women; the profits are mainly used for conspicuous consumption or re-investment in other "products" that can be sold relatively easily; and involves serious disregard for human rights.
2. The trade and development model – typical of Chinese traffickers
   This model is long-term and integrated; mainly affects men; generates significant funds that are then re-invested; and is somewhat less disrespectful of human rights than model one.
3. The supermarket model – typical of Mexican traffickers

This model typically builds on people smuggling to the USA at cheap rates; affects both males and females, with a particular focus on people with disabilities and minors; capital is mostly repatriated, though there is also considerable expenditure on corrupting Mexican border officials: this approach is particularly bad for human rights, and has a high rate of fatalities.

4. The violent entrepreneur model – common in the Balkans
   This involves a highly opportunistic approach, taking advantage of conflict and other forms of instability in the Balkan region; it mainly affects women; profits are invested both domestically and overseas: this is the worst model for human rights, since it is particularly violent.

5. Traditional slavery with modern technology – typical of Nigerian and other West African traffickers
   This model often uses voodoo as a way of exercising power over trafficked victims; it mainly affects women; most profits are laundered; and it is bad for human rights, in part because it often involves violence.

6. The rational actor model – the Netherlands typifies this approach
   This model applies to a receiving country in which brothels are legal and the state regulates the market for sex work; there is no need for money laundering, since the profits generated are considered legitimate and hence can be legally invested: this is the best model for human rights, since the state seeks to prevent sex-related THB through its regulatory role (brothels can be shut down if found to be using trafficked persons, which is assumed to act as a deterrent to "rational" brothel owners).

6.9 Neo-Marxist theories

One of the less common theoretical explanations for OC is neo-Marxism. In an introductory study such as this, it would be impossible to explore Marxism and its newer variants in any detail. For our purposes, a key aspect of the neo-Marxist approach is that OC is seen as ideological, whether or not it explicitly acknowledges this. This point is emphasised by Alfredo Schulte-Bockholt (2006: esp. 21–38), who focuses on the linkages in various parts of the world between OC and political elites (the state). He not only argues that such ties are all too common, but also relates them to the socio-economic contexts in which they are most prevalent. It is in part the close connections between and eventual integration of OC and political elites that leads him to maintain that the former adapt to the ideological perspective of the latter. Citing R.T. Naylor (1993), Schulte-Bockholt sees this convergence as a dynamic process that starts as predatory crime, which then becomes parasitical, and eventually mutates into a symbiotic relationship. In this final stage, there emerges a "criminalised state" – although this symbiosis can also exist beyond the individual state, at the transnational level. At this advanced stage, OC seeks to become more "respectable" (Schulte-Bockholt 2006: 35).[3]

In a thought-provoking part of his argument that resonates with part of our analysis in Chapter 4, Schulte-Bockholt maintains that totalitarian states are the best at controlling OC, but that they themselves are criminal; one reason why totalitarian (and authoritarian) states are in principle better equipped at dealing with OC is that they do not have to respect civil liberties and the rule of law as democracies do.

A neo-Marxist approach specifically to THB is adopted by Ronaldo Munck (2010). He argues that globalisation represents the culmination of capitalism, but that it has been accompanied by a marked increase in a new type of slavery. Whereas traditional slavery focused on formal ownership of human beings, the new form focuses on control of unfree labour, and does not seek formal (legalised) ownership. Apparently based more on wishful thinking than on reasoned and evidenced argument, Munck (2010: 25) concludes that "It is not modernist capitalism that will supersede slavery and other forms of unfree labour, but rather a post-modern socialism fit for the era of globalization."

6.10   Conclusions

By now it will be obvious that there is a rich arsenal of theories and variables that can help us better to understand OC, especially if we include the psycho-social and cultural approaches considered in Chapter 5 (further theories, as well as alternative analyses of some considered here, are in Kleemans 2014). It should also be clear that many of these theories overlap and are compatible with each other. In most actual cases of both OC and THB, a combination of the various theories (syncretism) is likely to provide the most convincing and satisfactory explanation of a given example. However, it must be emphasised that different theories and variables will provide the most convincing explanations for the scale and nature of particular examples of OC in particular contexts, and must be weighted differently. In one country, the poor socio-economic conditions will appear to be the dominant factor, whereas these conditions do not appear to be as salient in another country, in which cultural attitudes towards crime, or a weak state, provide a better explanation. Some theories are persuasive when applied to traditional, hierarchical OC syndicates, while others apply more to the recent, more flexible and loose network forms of OC, into which some of the traditional forms are mutating. In short, there is no "one size fits all" explanation of OC; when applying theoretical frameworks to analyse particular OC groupings, it is a case of "horses for courses".

NOTES

1 Only just over 49,000 applicants for refugee status – or some 11 per cent of the total number – had their applications recognised; but another 41,000 were granted admission on humanitarian grounds (all data from UNHCR 2013).

2 One *possible* exception to this general point is Somalia, with its reputation for piracy on the high seas (see McCarthy 2011: 203–16) – though this is not one of the states on which we have focused, and many would dispute that its piracy constituted TOC anyway.

3 Some of the OC groups analysed in this book have recently been discouraging their members from having tattoos, as part of the move towards greater respectability and lower visibility.

7 Combating organised crime: the role of states and IOs

The increasingly fluid structure and transnationalism of OC is rendering it more difficult for law enforcement agencies to combat it. But states and IOs are still the most significant agencies for addressing this issue. In the present chapter, a "5Ps" approach is adopted for analysing the methods available to government agencies and IOs in their fight against OC. This approach constitutes an expanded and modified version of the "3Ps" (prevention; prosecution; protection) approach adopted by the UN for addressing THB (see below), which was supplemented in 2009 by US authorities to become a "4Ps" approach (the existing three plus partnership); the fifth "P" is an appropriate addition to the existing framework:

- Prevention
- Protection (and assistance)
- Prosecution
- Partnership
- Publicity (awareness raising).

As with theories, so in considering official responses to OC and THB, an holistic approach is required. Approaches are separated here purely for the sake of clarity; in reality, it is necessary to combine as many as possible if progress is to be made in containing both OC and THB. Following a section on states is a section devoted to the role of IOs in fighting both OC and THB.

7.1 The state

7.1.1 Prevention

There are numerous ways in which states can work to prevent – or at least reduce – OC. The most obvious is through legislation. For instance, some states have made it illegal even to be a member of a group that has been proven to be involved in OC, whether or not an individual is accused of having committed a specific crime. A related approach is represented by the USA's 1970 RICO (Racketeer Influenced and Corrupt Organizations) Act. This was designed in part to close a loophole whereby OC bosses could order a subordinate to commit a contract killing, but could avoid prosecution themselves because of not being directly involved in the murder. One way in which RICO is considered to have been relatively successful is that those accused can be found guilty on the basis of previous behavioural patterns. The potential penalties are relatively harsh, up to US$25,000 fine or 20 years' imprisonment for each crime of which an accused is found guilty. Other countries with somewhat similar legislation include Australia, Canada and New Zealand.

Some countries have been accused of taking such legislation too far. Thus the Australian state of Queensland passed legislation in 2013 (the clumsily-named Vicious Lawless Association Disestablishment Bill) that requires judges to add a mandatory 15 years onto any prison sentence imposed on an OCG member, even if the crime is relatively minor and would normally incur a sentence of one year or less. Moreover, it is now illegal in Queensland for three or more members of an OCG to gather in public; this includes riding motorcycles in groups of three or more ("bikies" were the particular target of the legislation). As of mid-2015, one effect of this draconian legislation, which was being adopted in modified form in other Australian states but not Victoria, was that Australian bikie gangs were moving their bases to Victoria.

Since, according to many criminological theories, the primary motivation of OC is to generate profit, some countries have introduced laws that allow the state to sequester property that has been illegally acquired. Two such states have been among the worst in the world for illicit drug production and trafficking – Colombia and Mexico.

A common problem legislators face when drafting anti-OC laws is reaching agreement on definitions. It was shown in Chapter 1 how disparate and often vague definitions of OC are; obviously, the more diverse the definitions across jurisdictions, the more difficult it is to reach agreement on law enforcement across national boundaries. But agreeing on definitions is not the only problem. Another is that states often adopt radically different positions on how best to prevent particular forms of OC activity, and at what point an act becomes criminal. Within Australia, an individual can be charged in the Northern Territory with trafficking heroin if found in possession of two pure grams, whereas the threshold in Tasmania is 25 grams (Hughes et al. 2014: 2).

Many states and territories have established powerful law enforcement agencies specifically dedicated to combating OC. A prime example is Hong Kong. In addition to other more generalist agencies, it has an Organized Crime and Triad Bureau, a Criminal Intelligence Bureau, a Cyber Security and Technology Crime Bureau and a Narcotics Bureau within the Hong Kong Police Force, all of which focus on various aspects of OC activity. Sometimes, states also establish what are intended to be temporary task forces to address a particular problem or target a particular OC syndicate.

Given the focus in this book on THB as a major form of contemporary OC, it is worth considering how diverse the range of policies is on this. In some countries, such as Germany and the Netherlands, most forms of sex work are legal, and it is argued that this reduces the role of OC in prostitution. In Victoria (Australia), too, brothels can exist legally. But since it is relatively expensive and bureaucratic to obtain and retain a brothel licence, and given that owners of legal brothels are subject to numerous health and other regulations and have to pay taxes, there are also many illegal brothels. The anti-THB squad in Victoria has found it much easier to raid legal brothels, on the grounds of checking compliance, than illegal ones, since they need to apply for a court warrant in the latter case. Given this, it is easier to detect victims of THB in legal brothels than in illegal ones, which supports the argument of those who maintain that legalisation of prostitution is one way of reducing the involvement of OC in sex work.

However, some countries have adopted a radically different approach. Thus, while prostitution is legal in Sweden, using a prostitute's services is a criminal offence. The thinking behind this seemingly contradictory policy is that sex workers are victims and should not be treated as criminals, whereas those who use their services are not victims and should be punished. Swedish authorities usually claim that this policy has made Sweden a far less attractive destination for human traffickers, and has thus reduced this type of OC activity. Iceland and Norway have adopted similar legislation, which is nowadays known as the Nordic model.

Another way in which state authorities can work to prevent OC activity is to conduct risk (or vulnerability) assessments. For instance, they can assume – perhaps based on past experience – that they have a particular problem with TOC smuggling goods across their borders, so that they intensify their supervision at frontiers. They might also determine that a recent increase in taxes on cigarettes, or the change to unattractive packaging (as has happened in Australia), is likely to increase demand for smuggled cigarettes in original packets, so that they divert more resources into monitoring local markets, online advertising, and other areas where consumers are likely to look for cheap smokes in attractive packaging.

One situation particularly conducive to an increase in THB and that should trigger a rapid risk assessment is crisis. In the wake of both natural disasters and human conflict (wars), many people are desperate to escape to a safer location; this is a situation ripe for exploitation by people smugglers and human traffickers. There were several reports of a significant increase in THB from Nepal, mainly of women and children for sex work and forced labour, following the 2015 earthquake there (Clarke-Billings 2015; McQuade 2015). The conflicts in Iraq and Syria have also resulted in increased activity of people smugglers and human traffickers in the region, including of children to be coerced into becoming child-soldiers (US Department of State 2014: 210–13, 366–8).

Risk assessments are based on a level of abstraction. But there are more concrete ways in which law enforcement agencies can detect OC activity and thus reduce it. One is the use of sting operations or entrapment techniques. The former involves attempting to catch someone or a group already suspected of engaging in criminal activities in the act of committing a crime, whereas the latter goes further, and seeks to entice even normally law-abiding citizens to break the law. It should be fairly obvious that the latter raises more civil liberties issues than the former. Thus the Netherlands now permits sting operations but not entrapment, while Sweden has in theory prohibited both, though in practice it does engage in sting operations in certain circumstances, such as seeking to identify people attempting to purchase the services of a sex worker.

One of the potentially most useful ways in which law enforcement agencies can gather intelligence on – and eventually prosecute – OCGs is to plant undercover agents. A major problem with this is that it can be dangerous, even fatal, for such agents if the OCG discovers who they really are. The horrific torture, then murder, of US DEA agent

Enrique "Kiki" Camarena by corrupt police officers acting on behalf of Mexican drug traffickers in 1985 is an oft-cited example. Another potential problem is that it can be difficult to find appropriate agents if the OCG is based primarily on a particular ethnicity, especially if that ethnicity is not widely represented in the general community. The UK authorities could experience problems planting suitable agents in Albanian OCGs operating in Britain, for example.

Another potential source of information on OCGs is informants. But this method also has its problems. Some potential informants are illegal migrants running small businesses; while they may resent having to pay protection money to OCGs and fear such gangs, they may fear deportation even more, and so do not assist the police. A more common problem that applies in most jurisdictions is that many potential informants are themselves criminals – perhaps members of an OCG on which they are reporting – who are attempting to reduce or avoid punishment themselves; they will often seek a plea bargain in return for providing insider information on other criminals. Unfortunately, it is often difficult for the police to separate fact from fiction, or at least exaggeration, in such informers' reports. Witness protection programmes are sometimes offered to informants, but create the problems identified in Chapter 3.

In general, a far less problematic source of information is tip-offs from other police units. Such information can be based on local intelligence work involving, for instance, local observation of extravagant lifestyles. Suspicions can then be forwarded to dedicated intelligence agencies, such as financial intelligence units. In some states, these have the right and capacity to access individuals' bank accounts; suspicious transactions can then be further investigated.

In concluding this section on prevention, it is worth noting that states can deploy indirect methods. While consideration of all the possible methods is beyond the scope of this chapter, it is important to note that one of the most potentially effective is to reduce the likelihood of collusion between the police and OCGs. In addressing the police side of this equation, both stick (for example, heavy penalties, shaming) and carrot (better conditions) methods can be used, as can administrative ones such as rotation (in other words, regularly moving officers from unit to unit, so that there is less time and opportunity to develop "cosy" relationships) or the gender balance of forces. The state can also introduce radical measures. Thus Georgia from 2004 and Ukraine from

2015 both disbanded their (highly corrupt) traffic police services, and then created new ones; while it is too early to know whether or not this will drastically reduce corruption in the Ukrainian case, there is abundant evidence that it was highly successful – albeit at times rather arbitrary and roughshod – in the Georgian (Devlin 2010).

7.1.2   Protection

There are three main ways in which states can offer protection and assistance to victims of OCG activity – legal, economic and medical. While much of what follows is based primarily on what states can and do offer to victims of THB, some of these measures can also apply to other types of OC victim.

In terms of legal assistance, states can amend laws on labour – making it easier for THB victims to seek legitimate employment – and on sex work, so that trafficked persons, who have by definition been either coerced or deceived or both by traffickers, are treated as victims rather than criminals in states where prostitution is illegal. They can also provide free legal counselling, including in the trafficked person's own language.

States can help victims economically in various ways, including through the introduction of laws that give victims the right to claim compensation from OCGs. Another significant measure is to offer residence and training to THB victims, increasing the likelihood that they can start a new life. Often, states will pay to repatriate a victim. While many governments maintain this helps victims, this claim can be questioned; OCGs in the country of origin often re-traffic returned THB victims, or else such victims are treated back home as pariahs.

At least three types of medical assistance can be given by states to victims. The most obvious is to provide treatment for physical ailments. But many victims also need psychological help, which states can provide. Finally, states can play a major role in educating trafficked persons in the health issues relating to sex work. For example, they can explain why it is so important always to have safe sex (that is, with condoms) – although it must be acknowledged that many trafficked persons are coerced by their traffickers into having unsafe sex, thus increasing the likelihood of contracting HIV or other STDs.

Related to the issue of medical assistance is the question of how the use of illicit drugs should be treated. The Portuguese authorities have long seen drug use primarily as a health problem, and have preferred to rehabilitate recreational drug users rather than criminalise them, whereas most jurisdictions in Europe still treat illicit drug use primarily as a criminal offence.

7.1.3   Prosecution

In considering what states actually do and could do in terms of prosecution, one problem takes us back to the problems of definition. All too often, those accused of OCG activity avoid conviction because of technicalities, including ambiguous wording in legislation. But this is not the only problem. Another, which tends to become worse the more serious the crime, is securing evidence. It can be difficult to obtain convincing proof, perhaps because of police collusion with the criminals (for example, OCGs can bribe police officers to "lose" or doctor incriminating evidence). Another problem is that potential witnesses are often reluctant to testify in court against suspects. An obvious reason for this is that they have been threatened in some way. But there are other factors. Thus many victims of loan-sharking are worried they will be unable to secure alternative loans if they report or testify against the OCGs from whom they have borrowed funds at exorbitant rates.

Partly as a function of these various problems, some types of OC lead to far fewer prosecutions – and even fewer convictions – than would be expected or hoped for. This point is borne out by data provided in the US Department of State's annual *Trafficking in Persons Report*, which reveals that the ratio of convictions to prosecutions globally for THB is in most years only 50–60 per cent – although it has been as low as 35 per cent (2003) and as high as 74 per cent (2009). Globally, the number of prosecutions in 2014 was only slightly higher than in 2003, while the percentage of prosecutions resulting in convictions was markedly lower in 2014 than in 2005 and 2009, and almost the same as in 2004 (all calculations by the author on the basis of data in US Department of State 2007: 36, 2015: 48). Given that the estimates of the number of people being trafficked each year have not declined, with many analysts believing there has been an increase, there is clearly room for improvement in terms of prosecuting and convicting suspected traffickers.

Finally, it is also worth noting that while more than 30 countries, especially in Asia, impose the death penalty for serious cases of drug trafficking, few impose it for THB (China is a notable exception, allowing for capital punishment for both; Thailand introduced legislation in 2015 permitting the death penalty for certain types of THB). While we are not advocating capital punishment, the fact that the maximum penalty for THB in many countries is only 10–12 years' imprisonment demonstrates that THB is still not treated as seriously by many states as it should be; relatively lenient punishments if convicted help to explain the apparent growth of THB in recent years.

7.1.4 Partnership

There are several ways in which states can partner with other states and agencies to combat OC. For instance, they can share intelligence data. They can also mount joint operations. Italian and Albanian authorities did this in 2002; Operation Puna involved inter alia the use of high-speed boats to intercept Albanian traffickers crossing the Adriatic Sea, as well as subsequent joint prosecutions. According to Italian and Albanian authorities, this operation virtually stopped THB between the two countries.

States can also conclude extradition treaties with other states. However, this often proves to be difficult in practice. Some countries – Russia is a prime example – will not permit extradition of their own citizens. In other cases, jurisdiction A will not agree to an extradition treaty with jurisdiction B because A has banned the death penalty whereas B has not; this issue arises between EU member states and China. This particular problem is not insurmountable, however; the USA's federal authorities, as well as many US states, allow for the death penalty, but sometimes formally commit not to impose this if the EU will extradite a given suspect.

Joining international policing agencies, such as Interpol, Europol or Aseanapol, is another avenue. While the last of these has been much less active in fighting OC or THB than it could have been, both Interpol and Europol have been focusing on these in recent years; their role is considered below, under IOs. States can also help each other through knowledge and experience transfer. For example, the American FBI played the key role in the establishment of the International Law Enforcement Academy in Budapest in 1995; by 2015, more than 21,000 law enforcement officers from 85 countries had received training at this academy, including in how to counter OC.

States can also cooperate with domestic and international NGOs. Unfortunately, as demonstrated in the next chapter, there are very few NGOs dedicated to fighting OC. But there are many committed to assisting victims of THB, and states can fund and in other ways collaborate with these agencies.

Finally, states could be more cooperative than most are in attempting to standardise their definitions of OC. In principle, the fact that countries have signed up to UNCTOC and the Palermo Anti-Trafficking Protocol (see Chapter 1 and below) means that they should accept the definitions provided in those documents; a problem with this is that while the former defines various terms that relate to OC, it does not *explicitly* define the concept itself.

7.1.5   Publicity

One responsibility states should assume is to raise public awareness of OC and THB, and of the harm they do. Depending on the types of OC activity most salient in a given society, this might involve mass and social media campaigns warning of the dangers arising from illicit drugs, outlining the alternatives to obtaining loans at very high interest rates, explaining how ordinary citizens can protect themselves against cybercrime, and so on. The messages about the evils of OC and THB should begin in schools, but then be maintained, so that adults remain alert to the dangers of OC and the various forms of deception it employs.

7.2   IOs

There are various types of IO, notably global and regional, and these can play different roles in the fight against OC and THB. However, many aspects of their approaches are common: these include standard-setting; awareness raising; comparative information gathering (intelligence); and coordination.

7.2.1   Global IOs

The most significant global IO in terms of addressing OC and THB is the UN. This was established in 1945, when it comprised only 51 states; its membership now stands at 193 states, thus encompassing almost all the states and territories in the world (exceptions include Kosovo,

Taiwan and the Vatican). Its most important document concerning OC is the *UN Convention against Transnational Organized Crime* (UNCTOC, sometimes also called the Palermo Convention – see Chapter 1), which it describes as "the main international instrument in the fight against transnational organized crime" (UNODC 2015b). This became effective in September 2003.

The main UN document regarding THB is the *UN Protocol to Prevent, Suppress & Punish Trafficking in Persons, Especially Women & Children*; this is one of three Palermo Protocols, the other two being on people smuggling and on the manufacture and trafficking of firearms. The UN itself characterises its anti-trafficking protocol as "the first global legally binding instrument with an agreed definition on trafficking in persons" (UNODC 2015b). Like UNCTOC, to which it is appended, this was adopted in Palermo in 2000; it came into effect in December 2003.

The UN has a subdivision or agency that specialises in crime, including OC, namely the United Nations Office on Drugs and Crime (UNODC). This was established in 1997 – under a slightly different name, its current title dating from 2002 – by merging two agencies, and is based in Vienna. Its principal objectives are to be "a global leader in the fight against illicit drugs and international crime, and the United Nations lead programme on terrorism" (UNODC 2015c). It fulfils these roles through three main methods or "pillars": field-based technical cooperation projects (working with states to improve their anti-crime capacities); research and analytical work; and normative work (assisting states to ratify and implement international conventions, treaties, and so on). It considers TOC a major international security threat, and seeks to provide practical assistance in combating it. For example, it has provided advice since 2007 on how to deal with identity fraud, and in 2008 published a guide to witness protection in cases relating to OC. On UNCTOC's tenth anniversary, it announced its intention to produce a directory of OC cases and best practice in dealing with these; this manual, the *Digest of Organized Crime Cases*, was launched in 2012. One of the principal findings of the *Digest* (UNODC 2012: xiv) is that "Cases show that organized crime offences are at present characterized by transnationality, which complicates efforts to counter them."

The UNODC also plays a role in combating THB, and describes itself as "the only United Nations entity focusing on the *criminal justice element* of these crimes" (emphasis added, UNODC 2015d). Among its tasks are research and awareness-raising; at one time, its 2006 *Trafficking in Persons: Global Patterns* was its second most downloaded report, after one on drugs. Its latest report (UNODC 2014) provides detailed analysis of the trafficking situation both globally and by region for the period 2010–12 and for 128 countries; it explicitly highlights the role of OC in THB.

The UNODC has also produced useful practical publications and tools, such as a case law database to help courts standardise approaches, a Victim Translation Assistance Tool, and toolkits for combating THB. It also emphasises the role of community-led activities, and has funded projects for NGOs (for example, in Croatia, and in Bosnia and Herzegovina).

Another UN agency that focuses on THB, though only tangentially on OC, is the ILO (International Labour Organization). This was established in 1919, but has been a UN agency since 1946; it currently has 185 member states. Among its main objectives are to "Create greater opportunities for women and men to decent employment and income" and to "Enhance the coverage and effectiveness of social protection for all" (ILO 2001: 17 and 27); clearly, these can relate to working against THB. The ILO has produced a number of reports on THB, which can serve as inputs to states' policymaking.

An international agency that is more concerned with THB than OC per se is the International Organization for Migration (IOM). This was established in 1951, but has operated under its present name since 1989; it currently has 157 member states and 10 observer states. Its official mandate is to:

> promote orderly and humane migration, to help protect the human rights of migrants, and to cooperate with its Member States to deal with problems related to migration. One of the core challenges for IOM and its Member States is to combat trafficking in persons, which is an exploitative form of irregular migration involving the violation of the migrants' human rights. (IOM 2004: 1)

The IOM distinguishes the nature of its THB work in countries of origin and destination countries: in the former, it concentrates on awareness raising; capacity building and training; research/data collection; and law enforcement training. In the latter, its principal tasks are to provide shelter and protection; health assistance; and legal counselling (IOM 2004: 2). There are also some tasks that relate to both source and destination countries, including travel assistance. By 2015, the IOM had assisted more than 70,000 victims of THB since the mid-1990s.

The principal international police organisation is Interpol, which was established in 1923, currently has 190 member states, and sees its main objective as the enhancement of cooperation between police forces around the world. In terms of OC, Interpol tends to have targeted projects rather than a generic approach. For instance, in recent years it has focused specifically on "transnational Eurasian organised crime" ("Project Millennium", targeting OC originating from the FSU and the post-communist states of CEE); Asian OC (with a particular focus on its role in illegal football gambling and game-fixing under Operation Soga); and "Project Pink Panthers", targeting a string of jewellery raids in Europe, the USA and the Middle East, and believed to involve a loose network of groups that includes a significant number of gangsters originating from Yugoslav successor states.

Interpol uses the UN definition of THB and adopts four principal methods for addressing it. The first is operations and projects – concrete actions designed to dismantle trafficking networks. A recent example of such a project was Operation Bia II that was mounted in Ghana in May 2011. This involved cooperation between Interpol and the Ghanaian authorities to counter trafficking in children for slave-labour in the fishing industry. The joint operation freed 116 children between the ages of 5 and 17, and resulted in the conviction of 28 traffickers. The other three methods are the development and dissemination of technical tools and systems for sharing information globally; promoting partnerships by working across sectors; and organising events and conferences.

Unfortunately, as with other organisations considered in this chapter, Interpol operations are not invariably as successful as they could be. Thus, while Operation Infra-Red 1, which ran from July 2010 and was directed at serious crime including THB, resulted in a 30-year sentence for a Romanian trafficker nicknamed "Pig's Face" – he was sentenced in Spain in February 2012 – this was the *only* conviction, despite a number of arrests. Moreover, Interpol was attacked by cybercriminals in February 2012; it is clearly a matter of concern if even the world's leading international anti-crime organisation cannot protect itself against such attacks.

The Financial Action Task Force (FATF) also plays its role in fighting OC. This was established in 1989 by the G7, and nowadays works very closely with the Organisation for Economic Co-operation and Development (OECD). As of 2015, FATF comprises 34 member-states and two regional organisations (European Commission; Gulf Cooperation Council), though it also has a large number of associate members and observer organisations (for example, the IMF); Malaysia and Saudi Arabia enjoy observer status. FATF's main task is to counter money laundering. In addition to monitoring the implementation of AML policies in its member states, FATF produces reports and recommendations for governments and other agencies. In 1990, it published its "40 Recommendations" on combating money laundering; these were updated in 1996, 2001, 2003 and most recently in 2012 (FATF 2013). While these are of direct relevance to (T)OC generally, FATF has also focused specifically on THB, mainly on the methods by which traffickers can launder their ill-gotten gains (see FATF 2011).

7.2.2   Regional organisations

An important role within Europe is played by the Council of Europe (CoE). This was established in 1949, and originally comprised just ten member states; it now comprises 47 (all European states with the exception of Belarus and the Vatican). Since its main objective is the protection of "human rights, democracy and the rule of law" (CoE 2015), it is clear that it should have an interest in THB – and it does. In 1991, it published its *Recommendation No. R(91)11 on sexual exploitation, pornography and prostitution of, and trafficking in, children and young adults*, which the CoE itself describes as the "first international instrument dealing comprehensively with these matters" (CoE 2013: 36). This was followed in 2005 by the *Convention on Action against Trafficking in Human Beings*. One of the significant differences between the 1991 and 2005 documents is that the latter adopts a much broader perspective on THB, since it explicitly considers THB that does not relate to sex work as well as THB that does. This followed criticisms of both the CoE and Sweden for treating THB as if it pertained only to trafficking connected with sex work.

In 2005, the CoE announced that it would be setting up a body to monitor compliance with its Convention. This resulted in the establishment of GRETA (Group of Experts on Action against Trafficking in Human Beings), which began its work in 2009. GRETA monitors the THB situation within the EU and elsewhere in Europe (for example, Serbia,

Switzerland and Ukraine). One of its most important roles is to visit countries ("evaluation visits") and produce reports on its perceptions of the THB situation in those states; governments are then required to reply to the recommendations for improvement, and explain what they intend to do to address the problem areas identified by the GRETA team. GRETA produced a total of 35 reports in the first evaluation round that began in late-2010 and finished in 2014; a second round began in late-2014.

While the CoE does occasionally refer to (T)OC, this appears to be much less of a priority for it than THB. In 1959, it adopted its *European Convention on Mutual Assistance in Criminal Matters*, although this makes no direct reference to OC per se. Similarly, its 1990 *Convention on Laundering, Search, Seizure and Confiscation of the Proceeds from Crime* can clearly relate to (T)OC, but again does not explicitly refer to this. There is a fleeting reference to OC, however, in the appendix to the CoE's 2005 *Convention on Laundering, Search, Seizure and Confiscation of the Proceeds from Crime and on the Financing of Terrorism*.

But only to focus on publications would give an imbalanced picture of the CoE's efforts against (T)OC. For example, it has also cofunded (with the European Commission) the "CARPO" project that was designed to enhance police capacity in dealing with serious crime (which clearly included OC) in South Eastern Europe; this project ran 2004–7.

Despite its name – the Organization for Security and Co-operation in *Europe* – the OSCE comprises 57 participating states in three continents, viz. (North) America, (Central) Asia and Europe. Nevertheless, it sees itself as a regional organisation and focuses on European security issues. It was established in December 1994, replacing the CSCE (Conference on Security and Co-operation in Europe) that had been formed in the 1970s; it is headquartered in Vienna. One of its declared objectives is to combat THB. It has published a number of documents designed to assist in this, such as its 2003 *Action Plan to Combat Trafficking in Human Beings*, and a booklet that focuses on trafficking in domestic workers (OSCE 2010); the latter has not been a major concern for most IOs. In addition, the OSCE establishes missions in countries such as Montenegro and Bosnia-Herzegovina, and has what it calls a "presence" in Albania, where it launched a project in 2014 designed to counter trafficking of children.

Perhaps surprisingly, the EU does not have a dedicated document or statement on OC (see Bąkowski 2013a and the EU website – "Fight against organised crime"); the closest it comes to this is its *Council Framework Decision on the Fight Against Organised Crime* (2008). Rather, it has a large number of documents that concentrate on particular aspects of OC activities, such as cybercrime (for example, EU 2013) and child pornography (for example, EU 2011). Moreover, the EU is making serious efforts to harmonise member states' legislation – including on membership of an OC group and on the reporting of crime statistics (see Chapter 3) – and funds various projects designed to counter OC. It also played a major role in the establishment of the European Cybercrime Centre ("EC3") that commenced operations in January 2013 and is based within Europol (see below).

Focusing explicitly on the EU's efforts to combat THB, the European Parliament and the Council adopted the *Directive on preventing and combating trafficking in human beings and protecting its victims* in April 2011 (this replaces the 2002 Framework Decision), and an anti-THB *strategy* in June 2012 (European Commission 2012). The latter identifies five priorities:

A. Identifying, protecting and assisting victims of trafficking.
B. Stepping up the prevention of trafficking in human beings.
C. Increased prosecution of traffickers.
D. Enhanced coordination and cooperation among key actors and policy coherence.
E. Increased knowledge of and effective response to emerging concerns related to all forms of trafficking in human beings.

While these measures may prove to be effective, they were introduced in 2013–16, so it is too early to determine their impact.

However, the EU *has* already run various anti-THB projects, notably the three DAPHNE projects (DAPHNE I ran 2000–3; DAPHNE II was from 2004–8; DAPHNE III was in operation 2007–13) that were designed to protect women, young people and children from violence, including by traffickers (though the programme is broader than just that). These projects have provided funding – of almost 170 million euros – to NGOs involved in assisting THB victims (European Commission 2015).

A regional agency that has since 2010 been directly funded by the EU is Europol. This was established in 1999 – at which time it was funded by individual member states – but had predecessors, mainly for combating drug smuggling; it is based in the Hague. Europol's official mission is to "support its Member States in preventing and combating all forms of *serious international crime* and terrorism" (emphasis added, Europol 2015), which it does mainly by "supporting EU law enforcement authorities through *the exchange and analysis of criminal intelligence*" (emphasis added). Europol is aided by Eurojust, which was set up in 2002; it is tasked with the coordination of transnational investigations and prosecutions and the facilitation of extradition requests.

7.3   Conclusions

Even though the list of agencies considered in this chapter is far from exhaustive, it will be clear that there is a considerable number of agencies tasked with – usually inter alia – combating (T)OC and/or THB; most of these agencies' programmes are relatively new, with few pre-dating the early-1990s. It should also be clear that there is some division of labour among these agencies. Yet research suggests that the success rate of the various agencies, conventions, etc. has been limited. To take one example, and citing Bąkowski (2013a: 3) once more:

> The FD (the EU Council's 2008 Framework Decision – LTH) has met with strong criticism from various quarters. The Commission went as far as to make a formal statement ... that the FD did "not achieve the objective of the approximation of legislation on the fight against transnational organised crime as provided for in the Hague Programme". It is argued in this connection that the FD's provisions are so broad and flexible that they may lead to an over-extensive criminalisation. Moreover, most MS did not even have to change their legislation to formally comply with it. Indeed, the impact of the FD on aligning relevant national laws is considered to have been very limited. (for a detailed analysis of this issue see Calderoni 2012)

Why is this so? Bąkowski himself cites the need for unanimity among member states, which resulted in a compromise document. This point applies to many of the conventions and other formal statements considered in this chapter. But several other factors help to explain the limited success in combating OC and THB. One is that OCGs have often proven to be at least one step ahead of law enforcement agencies in terms of using technology; while there is no inherent reason for this, it has so far proved in practice to be the case.

On the other hand, a particularly thorny problem relating to the fight against OC and THB is that this can sometimes be hindered by the commitment to democracy and the rule of law. In many cases, one of the most effective methods for combating OC and THB is the use of undercover agents and other clandestine methods. But defenders of individual rights often criticise such approaches, on the grounds that they undermine civil liberties and grant excessive powers to the state. One other sensitive point is that a number of states use individuals' right to privacy as an excuse for permitting opaque banking practices (see Chapter 6); this plays into the hands of OC, as well as of corrupt officials and unethical corporations.

Turning now to consider THB specifically – there is no question that the legislative situation globally has improved significantly since the early-2000s. By 2009, 61 states had adopted dedicated anti-trafficking laws, 90 per cent of them since 2004 (UNIAP 2009). But this meant that a substantial majority of countries still did not have such laws. Moreover, passing laws and making a real difference is not the same thing. An example of the ineffectuality of much of the legislation is provided in a report on the compensation of victims that was based on an analysis of eight countries, in which the authors concluded that "the actual receipt of a compensation payment by a trafficked person is extremely rare" (Thompson and Jernow 2008: 10). The point about making a real difference is even more strongly endorsed by the findings of a detailed German comparative empirical analysis of the implementation of anti-THB legislation, which concluded that:

> While anti-trafficking efforts improved worldwide over the last decades, the negligence of policy makers in protecting victims of human trafficking has persisted. . . . In addition . . . the recent decline in enforcement efforts points out that there is a policy gap between the adoption of anti-trafficking legislation and the actual realization of the written policy . . . weak enforcement is a fundamental problem . . . because negligence in enforcing anti-trafficking measures decreases costs and risks to human traffickers, which, in turn, increases their incentives to commit the crime of human trafficking. (Cho 2015: 94)

A new (March 2015) law that could serve as a model for other countries' legislation in the future is the UK's Modern Slavery Act, which the British government has promoted as the first of its kind in Europe and one of the first in the world. But the British law has been a long time coming, and is still an exception globally. Moreover, the NGO Anti-Slavery has identified what it sees as certain deficiencies in the Act, such as inadequate protection of migrants in domestic service. It also remains to be seen how effectively and energetically the law will be applied in practice.

In attempting to understand why states continue to be criticised for often doing too little too late, we must unfortunately ask some awkward – some would say cynical – questions. Is it really in the interests of source states to raise public awareness about the problem, for instance? After all, such states are usually relatively poor, or have a large impoverished section of the population – and if the state no longer has to assume any responsibility for some of the poorest and least educated members of society because they have been trafficked to more affluent states, the state has offloaded some of its problems. But do affluent states also have a vested interest in turning a blind eye to THB, or at least sweeping it under the carpet?

In a 2010 analysis (Holmes 2010b: esp. 181–8), the present author argued that trafficked persons are subjected to "quadruple victimisation". The first three forms are by private individuals (the traffickers; complicit family members and friends; those who purchase or use the products and services of trafficked people), corrupt officials, and the media (which, for example, sometimes present romanticised images of OC and publish titillating photos of trafficked sex workers).[1] But in some ways the greatest opprobrium attaches to the fourth source of victimisation, the state – whether developed or developing – itself. There are at least six ways in which states can, albeit sometimes unwittingly and unintentionally, contribute to the persecution of THB victims and in some cases indirectly assist (T)OC. These are:

- Providing inappropriate support – notably immunity from prosecution – for state officials suspected of exploiting THB victims in various ways.
- Prioritising the interests of the state (for example, border security) over the human rights of THB victims.
- Treating trafficked persons as criminals rather than victims (for example, if such persons have been smuggled into a country, or have engaged in sex work where prostitution is illegal: a 2015 report in the British media details how some Vietnamese children

who have been trafficked to the UK have been sent to detention centres rather than assisted – Kelly and McNamara 2015).
- Providing inadequate or no education to the state's officers in what is supposed to be victim-supportive legislation.
- Being unduly slow and bureaucratic in dealing with allegations of THB (so that the victims have been expelled from the country before their cases have been resolved, or giving their traffickers enough time to leave that state).
- Subjecting THB victims to more stress than is necessary, such as requiring them to confront their alleged traffickers face-to-face in court, or insisting on repatriation to the victim's home-country when the victim has made it clear that this would be detrimental or even dangerous.

In short, states frequently put their own interests and those of what they perceive to be the interests of their citizens (electorates) and officers above those of trafficking victims. All too often, states place considerable emphasis on prevention and prosecution (that is, criminal) dimensions of THB and not enough on protection. While this criticism may seem unduly harsh, it is worth noting that, in 2010, the NGO Anti-Slavery called the new anti-trafficking laws in the UK "not fit for purpose" and claimed that they breached the Council of Europe's anti-trafficking convention. In some cases, it even seems as if some IOs are more interested in *appearing* to be doing something by creating more agencies and employment rather than *actually* helping victims in substantive ways.

Merely criticising or being cynical is ultimately negative, however, and in itself does nothing to help trafficking victims. A more positive and helpful approach is to suggest other methods that might improve the lot of trafficked persons. It has been argued by many ever since the prohibition era in the US in the 1920s and early-1930s that banning the sale of goods or services for which there is considerable consumer demand will encourage the growth of OC. On the basis of this, it could be argued that legalising drugs or sex work should reduce the salience of OC. Let us briefly explore both propositions.

According to an analysis published by the Cato Institute, the decriminalisation of illicit drugs in Portugal from 2001 has not led to any increase in drug usage (for many types of illicit drug, Portuguese rates are among the EU's lowest and have declined slightly), but has dramatically improved drug-related problems, such as deaths from overdoses and STDs. In short, decriminalisation has been judged a resounding success, especially compared with the tough criminalisation approach adopted by other countries both within and beyond the EU, such as the USA (Greenwald 2009; Anderson 2012; Hollersen 2013). Given that decriminalisation lessens the attraction of drug-dealing to OC, the empirical evidence suggests that Portugal's approach to illicit drugs should be seriously considered, and probably emulated, by other states.

The decriminalisation of sex work is a more contentious issue. On one hand, pursuing such a policy should reduce the role of OC. On the other hand, doing so can also be seen to "normalise" – make more socially acceptable – the sale of sex, and thus increase demand; if demand exceeds supply (that is, of people consciously deciding to be sex workers), then OCGs may still play a significant role as traffickers. Comparing the experiences of Victoria (Australia) and Sweden is revealing on this issue. Most forms of sex work except street-walking were legalised – not merely decriminalised – in Victoria in 1986 and, according to one source, this increased the number of trafficked sex workers (Yen 2008: 680–2). On the other hand, and as noted above, it is often easier for law enforcement agencies in rule-of-law based states to raid legal brothels than illegal ones, since they can ensure compliance in the former, but need a warrant to raid the latter. Moreover, HIV rates are very low among Victoria's legal sex workers, who pay taxes and who are arguably better protected against client violence than are Swedish prostitutes, since the sort of men who will risk a prison sentence for having sex with a prostitute are more likely to be violent, including insisting on unsafe sex. In short, the impact of decriminalising or legalising prostitution on OC and THB rates is unclear, and often depends on specific circumstances in a given country.[2]

At the end of the day, one of the most important factors in combating both (T)OC and THB is political will and capacity. But since this refers not only to states and IOs, but also to civil society and individuals, it is a factor more appropriately considered in our concluding chapter.

NOTES

1 Readers interested in the *negative* role the media sometimes play in the fight against THB should look up the impact of *Newsweek's* criticisms of Somaly Mam in 2014.

2 But see Chapter 8 for evidence that many relevant IOs and TNGOs now favour decriminalisation of sex work.

8 Combating organised crime: the role of other agencies

While most citizens believe that combating OC crime is the state's responsibility, many other agencies can and should play a role. Indeed, in highly corrupt states, where officials regularly collude with OC gangs, the role of non-state agencies is crucial. The focus in this chapter is on the potential and sometimes actual role of civil society and individuals.

8.1 The role of civil society, domestic and international

As with so many concepts in the social sciences, specialists cannot agree on exactly what civil society means. Sidestepping this debate, we shall here simply specify the various agencies we consider to constitute civil society, and then examine the role each can play in countering OC. For our purposes, civil society comprises:

- The mass media;
- The business sector;
- Domestic and transnational NGOs; and
- Other components, including social media.

In addition, there is consideration here of the role demonstrations can and sometimes do play, before finally examining what each of us as individuals can do.

8.1.1 The mass media

While social media are growing almost exponentially in significance in all sorts of areas and ways – including the spread of OC and means to combat it – the mass media, both print and electronic, still play a major role in raising public awareness of various kinds of problem and possible solutions to these. Unfortunately, many media focus heavily on the former, and far too little on the latter. In most capitalist democracies, the media are relatively free to investigate and report on OC; since commercial media need to be profitable to survive, many of them operate according to the maxims "bad news is good news" (in other words, since sales tend to increase if there are reports of a serious problem such as a natural disaster or gangland warfare) and "if it bleeds, it leads".

A useful approach to the possible roles played by the mass media is to adopt and adapt Rodney Tiffen's (1999) analysis in terms of five canine models or metaphors. The first and ideal one is for the media to act as a watchdog, investigating and reporting on all important events and advocating change if necessary. Unfortunately, the media are in many countries more like muzzled watchdogs, Tiffen's second type. In some, censorship prevents them from playing their proper watchdog role. But Tiffen identifies another way in which the media can be muzzled – viz. defamation laws. In some countries, the law is so heavily skewed towards the rights of those against whom allegations are made that most media outlets are extremely apprehensive about making negative claims, including about OC and THB. Moreover, we can add that so many journalists who have been investigating OC have been murdered that it is hardly surprising that many prefer not to report OC activity. Tiffen's third metaphor is the lapdog, meaning that the media obey their political masters; if the latter choose not to criticise OC or THB – perhaps because they are colluding with OC, or feel unable or unwilling to address THB – then the media will similarly be largely silent about these phenomena. The fourth possibility is the yapping pack. Here, the media do not engage in serious investigative journalism, and copy each other in reporting mostly trivial events; the media in such a situation are more bark than bite. Finally, the media can play the role of a wolf. This is the most dangerous type of reporting, in which the media are careless about investigating sources, but frequently publish or broadcast stories that undermine public confidence in the system and increase fear.

As noted in the previous chapter, the mass media often play a negative role in reporting (T)OC and THB. Gangsters and thugs are frequently portrayed as "macho" tough guys, which impresses many readers. But the media could – and fortunately often do – play a more positive role by engaging in serious investigative journalism, ensuring that reports portray OC as a menacing, illegal and illicit activity, and treating THB as a form of slavery. Among the many media that play such a positive role are the British Broadcasting Corporation (for example, BBC

2015b), the *Guardian* newspaper (for example, Kelly and McNamara 2015), the *New York Times* (for example, Editorial Board 2015), CNN (see their "Freedom Project")[1] and the *Frankfurter Allgemeine Zeitung* (for example, Rojkov 2015).

8.1.2   The business sector

There are various ways in which businesses can play a role in combating OC. One is to refuse to pay protection money; if this appears to be too dangerous, they can blow the whistle on the gang threatening them. A problem here is that the police in some countries are so corrupt, and colluding with the OC gangs, that businesses may fear reporting; this is one reason why states must work much more energetically to combat police corruption (see Holmes 2014b). Businesses can also be much more wary of goods and services offered to them at considerably cheaper prices than normal; the likelihood is that such goods or services have been either stolen or else produced by trafficked labour. Companies that trade with overseas suppliers can commit to "fair trade" products. For example, following a campaign by Stop the Traffik (see below) to fight against child slavery in the cocoa growing countries of West Africa, notably Côte d'Ivoire, a number of chocolate manufacturing companies, including Cadbury and Swiss Noir, have in recent years committed to using fair trade sources.

Businesses can also monitor their overseas suppliers and their own overseas factories to ensure that workers are being treated properly in terms of wages, working conditions, and so on; if they suspect this is not the case, they can either do something themselves about it or else whistleblow.

In practice, there is still a long way to go in terms of businesses "doing the right thing". In 1999, a number of companies – most of them household names – were sued for exploitation of Chinese and Filipino sweatshop workers producing goods on the US island of Saipan in the Pacific; although the island had different (more lax) labour legislation from the rest of the US, it meant that these companies could legitimately label their products "Made in the USA". This was the first example of this type of action against companies. Several of them – including Tommy Hilfiger, Calvin Klein, Sears, Roebuck and Wal-Mart – settled out of court in 2000. But Gap, Levi Strauss and Target, for example, chose to contest the allegations. In May 2002, a US court ruled that Saipan workers had the right to sue the companies that had not settled, and blocked these companies from challenging the settlement Hilfiger and eighteen other US retailers had already reached.

The case was finally closed in 2004, when all but one of the companies originally accused of subjecting workers to "involuntary servitude" agreed to a US$20mn settlement (all from Business & Human Rights Resource Centre 2014). The one exception was Levi Strauss, against which the case was dropped; it had made attempts in the 1990s to improve labour conditions on the island, and in frustration stopped purchasing products manufactured in Saipan in 2000. While this case against US retailers and manufacturers does not clearly relate to OC, the treatment of many Saipan workers did virtually amount to slave labour, with the reference to "involuntary servitude" making this clear.

In practice, many companies still need to be more cautious when sourcing their goods. A 2014 investigation by Britain's *Guardian* newspaper (Hodal et al. 2014) discovered that slave labour was being used indirectly by Thai companies supplying prawns to, among others, the world's four largest retail chains (the French Carrefour; Britain's Tesco's; and the US companies Costco and Walmart). In this case, however, the retailers soon responded positively, some (for example, Tesco's) attending a meeting in Thailand in July 2014 to address the matter, while others (for example, Carrefour) broke their contracts with the Thai supplier (Kelly 2014).

But it is not enough to suspect only overseas product sources; THB means that there are often trafficked labourers in highly developed countries. Leading British supermarket chains such as Tesco's and Sainsbury's, for instance, have been accused of purchasing eggs and chickens at suspiciously low prices from British suppliers that were allegedly using trafficked labourers from Lithuania working in England (Lawrence 2012). In 2015, some of these Lithuanians sued the Kent-based company that had trafficked them and been supplying major supermarket and fast-food chains in what the *Guardian* newspaper described as "the first case of a UK company being taken to court for claims relating to modern slavery" (Lawrence 2015).

Recognising the need for various private sector agencies to play a greater role in combating the use of trafficked labour, the British government announced in 2014 that it was about to introduce new rules aimed at making them far more responsible for their purchasing policies (Travis 2014); an annual reporting requirement for large companies was included in the March 2015 Modern Slavery Act mentioned in Chapter 7 and invoked in the case cited in the previous paragraph.

So far in this section, the focus has been on what businesses can do vis-à-vis other businesses (notably suppliers), and what companies can be required to do by governments. But the business sector in most countries has a powerful voice, and could use its influence more energetically to persuade governments to adopt tougher policies designed to combat OC. In short, businesses could use their muscle – notably via lobbying – not only to pursue their own interests, but also to promote better law enforcement, more support for OC victims, and so on.

Before concluding this section on the role of the business sector, it is imperative to consider explicitly the role of banks. Banks are frequently far more concerned with making large profits than in playing the socially responsible role they should be playing. Their often highly complicit role – notably in money laundering, evading sanctions imposed on "rogue" states, and "facilitation", all of which can play right into the hands of OC – has recently been explored in detail (Platt 2015).

The advantages of money laundering to OC and the potential role of banks in this are clear; HSBC is just one of several banks that have been heavily fined by US authorities for their role in laundering OC funds (in the HSBC case, from Mexican drug cartels). But those relating to sanctions busting are less obvious; an actual example will clarify this. While the transition to post-communism from Communism between 1989 and 1991 was relatively peaceful in most countries, it was not in former Yugoslavia. Since much of the West placed the primary blame for the violent break-up of Yugoslavia on Serbia, sanctions were imposed on it. But OC was largely able to circumvent these, smuggling in necessities such as oil, and then depositing their profits into banks that asked few if any questions concerning the origin of such funds. Finally, "facilitation" refers primarily to the role some banks play in assisting clients to evade paying taxes; this, too, can be very beneficial to OC, especially in those aspects of their operations that relate to the legal economy.

8.1.3   Domestic and transnational NGOs

Unfortunately, there are very few NGOs primarily concerned with combating (T)OC. This is in part because of fear that gangs would use or threaten violence against such organisations. However, this is not to suggest that there are *no* anti-OC NGOs. An example is the German Mafia – Nein Danke. This was formed in 2007 in reaction to gang warfare in Duisburg that left six members of a 'Ndrangheta clan dead; it was formally registered as an NGO in 2009 – in the same year as one of its initiatives, an agreement between German law enforcement agencies and the Italian community in Berlin, was commended by the EU as an example of best practice in linking security agencies and civil society. Mafia – Nein Danke provides the following list of its activities:

- Counter the activities of the Mafias in Germany;
- Raise public awareness that Mafias operate on an international level, and therefore a joint European legislation must be implemented;
- Monitor the activities of the Mafias in Germany;
- Collaborate with journalists, magistrates, and police who fight the Mafias in Germany;
- Organise educational projects promoting the importance of legality; and
- Keep alive the memory of heroes and victims fighting the Mafias.[2]

One of the best-known anti-OC NGOs, and one with which this German NGO cooperates, is Libera. This was established in Italy in 1995 "with the purpose of involving and supporting all those who are interested in the fight against mafias and organized crime" (Libera 2015) and is based in Rome, with branches in Brussels and Paris. Libera has achieved a number of successes, such as having played a role in the adoption of an Italian law that grants to third parties property that has been confiscated because it was acquired through illegal means; the third parties then return them to the community for socially useful purposes, such as growing agricultural products.

"Meld Misdaad Anoniem" ("Report Crime Anonymously") – based in Hoevelaken in the Netherlands and established in 2002 – provides a hotline for anonymous reports on "serious" crime, including (T)OC and THB. It assures anonymity at all times, and encourages "phone callers to report known or suspected cases of money laundering and other OC activities". It announced in 2014 that it had received and passed on to relevant agencies 34 per cent more anonymous tips on extortion, money laundering and criminal assets than in 2012. Like most other anti-crime NGOs, it works closely with state agencies and IOs, including Interpol.

One area in which NGOs should be less fearful of OC – at least of physical violence – is cybercrime. Yet the development of anti-cybercrime NGOs is still at an early stage. An interesting example from Canada, however, is the Society for the Policing of Cyberspace ("POLCYB"), established in 1999. POLCYB's stated principal objective is to "enhance international partnerships among public and private professionals to prevent and combat crimes in cyberspace".[3] It does this largely through the facilitation of information-sharing related to cybercrime. POLCYB also strives to raise public awareness of cyber-crime, for instance through public education fora.

Although evidence has been provided here of NGOs that address OC, those dedicated specifically to fighting OC are still rare. The situation is much better when we turn to consider NGOs that address THB. Such NGOs exist all over the world, including the Open Arms Foundation in Colombia (operative since 1991), Beyond the Streets in the UK (established in 1995), Eden House in Thailand (set up in 1997), Project Respect in Australia (founded in 1998) and the Angel Coalition (of 43 NGOs, established in 1999) in Russia. While most of these focus on trafficking victims coerced into the sex industry, several also work to assist other trafficking victims. Many of these cooperate with similar organisations in other countries; some are connected to the church (mostly Christian), while others are fully secular.

In addition to the usual methods used for awareness-raising, the German (and now also Swiss) NGO Terre des Femmes, founded in 1981, adopted an innovative approach in their 1999 campaign "Men Show the Way". Rather than simply criticise men who used prosti-tutes, this NGO attempted to raise awareness among clients ("johns") that many sex workers are coerced into their work and subjected to violence, and encouraged them to report known or suspected trafficking victims or victims of violence. Terre des Femmes claims that this project was largely successful (Howe 2005: 101).

However, most such agencies are primarily concerned with helping trafficking victims, rather than combating the traffickers. A typical example is the NGO Animus Association, which has since 1998 been implementing the La Strada (see below) programme in Bulgaria. It lists its main activities as support for trafficked persons (for example, providing shelters/safe houses); education; and advocacy. It also provides a useful "checklist" of the types of activities in which anti-trafficking NGOs can engage:

- Counselling
- Prevention
- Rehabilitation
- Research
- Training
- Anti-Human Trafficking
- Legal Assistance.

Like other agencies involved in combating THB, NGOs face various problems. The most obvious is funding; unfortunately, too few agencies have a vested interest in financially supporting the work of such NGOs. Second, and closely related to the first point, is the problem of independence; since many anti-THB NGOs depend heavily on states and other official agencies for much of their income, they often have to conform to conditions with which they at least partly disagree. Two countries that have in recent times been increasingly interfering in the work of NGOs are Russia and China. The former introduced a new law in 2012 that required NGOs that receive any foreign funding to register as "foreign agents", a term that has a very negative connotation in Russia, essentially being equated with espionage. Possibly emulating the Russians, China was debating a rather similar law – "Governing Foreign NGOs" – in 2015, and was expected to pass this by the end of the year.

Third, some NGOs are also concerned about threats from (T)OC. However, the head of a German anti-THB NGO interviewed by the author argued that OC would not normally threaten NGOs, for two reasons. One is that any threat of violence would in many countries lead to a far more significant police response than if OC were simply being a nuisance and keeping a low profile. This said, in the many countries in which the police regularly collude with OC, the state's response would be much less encouraging than where the rule of law is more firmly established. The other reason is a depressing one. As the NGO director pointed out, the supply of trafficked women is almost limitless; if an NGO manages to save five women in a week, and the OC gang can readily acquire ten more, why would the traffickers bother trying to retrieve those they had lost, thereby potentially attracting the attention of law enforcement bodies?

Focusing now on transnational or international NGOs – during a meeting with NGOs in October 2010, UNODC Executive Director Yury Fedotov thanked them and civil society organisations generally for the role they were playing in the fight against TOC, as well as for the significant support they were providing to victims. The meeting had been convened by the Vienna Alliance of NGOs on Crime Prevention and Criminal Justice. This was established in 1980 and is closely allied with the UN. In addition to the few domestic anti-OC NGOs already considered, various TNGOs also play their role. Among the best known is FLARE (Freedom Legality And Rights in Europe), which is a coalition of 50 NGOs from 26 European countries and Russia; it was set up in 2008 and describes its role as "the social struggle against mafias and transnational organised crime" (FLARE 2015: 1). Another well-known TNGO is the Crime Stoppers International Foundation that has been in existence since the 1970s, and which encourages citizens to report crime to law enforcement agencies. However, fighting OC is only one part of Crime Stoppers' much broader mandate to combat almost all forms of crime. In short, the dearth of anti-OC NGOs noted at the national level is – unfortunately – replicated at the international level.

Let us now consider TNGOs that focus explicitly on THB. As was the case with the domestic anti-THB NGOs, the situation here is much better than that of TNGOs specifically directed against OC. There are several explicitly international anti-trafficking NGOs. One such is La Strada International, founded in 1995 and now having branches in eight European states (Belarus, Bulgaria, Czechia, Republic of Macedonia, Moldova, the Netherlands, Poland and Ukraine); it is headquartered in Amsterdam. Other TNGOs include Anti-Slavery International (based in London, founded in 1839, and describing itself as the world's oldest international human rights association), Stop the Traffik (established 2006, headquartered in London), and Not For Sale (established 2007, based in San Francisco). Among the numerous tasks identified by TNGOs is fundraising, while their methods include advocacy (mainly to states and IOs); consultancy (to relevant decision-makers, such as legislators); coordination (of both domestic NGOs and with IOs); education and general awareness raising; and research.

Most of these TNGOs are committed to fighting THB of all sorts. But another well-known one – the Coalition Against Trafficking in

Women (CATW – established 1988, and based in New York) – is concerned exclusively with female victims of trafficking, particularly those trafficked for the purposes of sexual exploitation. Among the many techniques it has used is to mount protests as a way of raising public awareness. For example, it organised a demonstration against HBO (Home Box Office) in 2008 for broadcasting *Cathouse*, a documentary television series about the lives of sex workers in a Nevada brothel. This action demonstrates how CATW sees legal prostitution as conducive to THB – a position many professionally involved in anti-THB work believe confuses the distinction between sex work by people who have consciously chosen to engage in it and others who have been forced into it.

TNGOs sometimes collaborate with each other, states and IOs on particular projects designed to help the victims of THB (and thus of OC). A recent example is COMPACT, which began in 2008. This is an initiative of La Strada International and Anti-Slavery International, and involves 14 European countries (eight post-communist states and six West European ones, but not Sweden or the Netherlands). Its primary objective is to improve the compensation situation for trafficking victims: the methods it uses are to engage in research; mount test cases; develop guidelines for professionals; run awareness campaigns; and international advocacy.

Unfortunately, most TNGOs suffer from the same problems as their domestic counterparts – funding, interference from sponsors, and sometimes also threats. This said, some find that linking up with a major IO can bring significant benefits. Thus Stop the Traffik has worked closely with the UN, particularly the UNODC, since 2008, apparently to the real advantage of both sides.

8.1.4   Other components of civil society

In addition to the mass media, the business sector and NGOs, other components of civil society also have their role to play. One is universities and research institutes, which can provide detailed information on both OC and THB. Among the best-regarded for researching the former are the Centre for Information and Research on Organised Crime (CIROC) in the Netherlands; the Max Planck Institute for International Criminal Law (Germany); Transcrime – The Joint Research Centre on Transnational Crime (Italy); Bulgaria's Center for the Study of Democracy; and the Terrorism, Transnational Crime and Corruption Center (TraCCC) – headquartered just outside Washington DC, but also having branches in Georgia (1) and Russia (4), and affiliates in Ukraine (2).

Universities can also play an important role beyond researching and publishing on OC and THB. In early-1998, student activists and university authorities at Duke University in North Carolina adopted an anti-sweatshop code of conduct. This committed the university to doing all it could to ensure that Duke-related apparel was not produced in sweatshops. This approach was rapidly adopted by many North American tertiary and secondary level educational institutions, which joined forces to create United Students Against Sweatshops (USAS), also in 1998. This now has an estimated 250 plus branches across the US and Canada, and is committed both to stopping the use of forced or blatantly exploited labour (particularly children), and raising public awareness of this problem (on this movement's early days see Featherstone 2002).

A generally less structured, but still often effective, form of activism against OC or THB or both is demonstrations and protests. Unfortunately, some of the very few protests relating to OC have been mounted by citizens identifying particular ethnic groups as responsible for it. For instance, a demonstration held in Bulgaria in October 2011 explicitly blamed local members of the Roma community for the rise in organised crime. Luckily, however, the majority of such demonstrations are not racist, but instead target OC itself, or else specific OC groupings. There were significant public protests in Italy against the Mafia following the murders of judges Falcone and Borsellino (Siegel and van de Bunt 2012: vi), for instance, while Japanese citizens appear to be increasingly prepared to demonstrate against the Yakuza (Rankin 2012).

There have also been demonstrations against THB. One was held in Prague in 2011, when Czechs protested against the use of forced labour in the logging industry. But one of the best-known group of activists in this field is the feminist cooperative FEMEN. This was originally formed in Ukraine in 2008, inter alia to raise awareness of THB and domestic violence against women, but soon captured the interest of the mass media worldwide. This was primarily because of the group's unconventional way of protesting: they usually demonstrate topless, precisely as a way of drawing attention to themselves and thus to the cause they espouse. The Ukrainian authorities soon clamped down on the group, which responded by moving its headquarters to Paris. They have demonstrated in various cities in Europe and beyond, including Brussels, Hanover, Kiev, London, Montreal, Paris and Sofia. Not all of these protests are explicitly about THB (the church and the fashion industry are other favourite targets); but coverage of these events leads many members of the public to seek more information on the group, which in turn raises awareness of their anti-THB and anti-sex work stance.

8.2   Individuals

The notion that it is only states, IOs and other organisations of various kinds, or even group protests, that can resist OC and THB is wrong. Individuals also have an important role to play. One important group is influential show business and other personalities, who can act as role-models to others. Among the famous people who have publicly condemned THB, for example, are the British actress Emma Thompson (in 2007) and the American singer Alicia Keys, via Twitter in 2011. In 2015, a number of famous personalities – including Meryl Streep, Anne Hathaway and, again, Emma Thompson – signed an open letter to Amnesty International (AI) urging it not to support decriminalisation of sex work, partly on the grounds that to do so would play into the hands of human traffickers.

This particular attempt failed. In August 2015, AI adopted a policy to join many other IOs and TNGOs – including the World Health Organization, the ILO and Anti-Slavery International – in support of the decriminalisation of consensual adult sex work. This decision was based on research in many countries over a two-year period, which led AI to conclude that, on balance, the human rights of sex workers, including trafficked ones, would be better served if sex work were legal than illegal. However, AI also emphasised that it was not supporting pimps, which would include traffickers:

> To be clear, *our policy is not about protecting "pimps"* (emphasis in original). Amnesty International firmly believes that those who exploit or abuse sex workers must be criminalized. But the reality is laws which criminalize "brothel-keeping" and "promotion" often lead to sex workers being arrested and prosecuted themselves. In Norway we found evidence that sex workers were routinely evicted from their homes under so-called "pimping laws". In many countries of the world, two sex workers working together for safety is considered a "brothel". (Murphy 2015)

The setback for the actors mentioned above should not be interpreted as a sign of the futility of publicly agitating for authorities to assume greater responsibilities in defending human rights and countering OC. Individuals still have an important role to play in raising awareness of the injustices of THB, and of the often cruel methods used by OC. Advocacy of the decriminalisation of sex work should *not* be construed as being in any way supportive of either OC or THB. Rather, it should be seen as opting for the lesser of two evils, and designed to help those who have been coerced by criminals into slave labour.

One group that could play an important role in raising awareness of THB is sports stars, since they are often looked up to by young, impressionable people. While such stars have increasingly criticised drug abuse (which, if effective, can reduce drug trafficking and hence OC's role in this), there is little in the way of anti-THB campaigning among them. One notable exception to this point is the group of 17 major baseball players in the US who publicly committed to Not for Sale's "Free2Play" campaign from 2011; many more sports stars could and should follow suit.

As social media become an increasingly significant means of communication between large numbers of people, blogs can also be a valuable source of awareness-raising about OC and THB. A good example is the work of the German Juergen Roth on CEE OC, available on both Twitter[4] and Facebook.[5]

Another way in which social media could play a positive role in countering THB – as one of the major activities of contemporary OC – is to attempt to change dominant attitudes in conservative male-dominated cultures towards pre- and extra-marital sex. In many cultures, men still want to marry a virgin, while there are strict taboos on adultery. However, men in such societies still have libidos, and so will often turn to prostitutes for release of sexual tension; this increases demand for sex workers, which can in turn increase the demand for trafficked persons.

In theory, citizens – all of us – can stop purchasing extremely cheap goods unless there is proof that they have not been produced by trafficked workers. Unfortunately, such proof is often impossible to obtain. Moreover, many people would continue to purchase "bargain price" goods anyway, whatever they are told about the source of such products. We can also stop buying illicit drugs, since these are almost always connected with OC; unfortunately, most users of recreational drugs know this, yet continue to pay criminals to feed their habits. As long as so many citizens continue to purchase goods and services they know or suspect have been provided by OC, the fight against the latter will be severely hampered.

8.3   Conclusions

By now, it will be clear that all branches of civil society, as well as all of us as individuals, can play their part in combating OC and THB. But has much been achieved? At first glance, the limited and ultimately questionable data on OC and on THB suggest that the fight against both is proving to be a Sisyphean task: rates of many kinds of OC activity do not appear to be improving, and some are clearly worsening. But it has also been demonstrated that awareness of both OC and THB has been rising, and that there are now many ways in which institutions and societies can and do fight back. Moreover, can we be certain that OC or THB rates would not have been even higher had there been no activism? Expressed another way, while the fight against the various manifestations of OC has not been won, this cannot be used as an excuse not to at least maintain, and preferably intensify, our efforts against it. To do so would mean that OC had won.

NOTES

1   http://thecnnfreedomproject.blogs.cnn.com/ (accessed 25 November 2015).
2   http://mafianeindanke.de/home_en/ (accessed 25 November 2015).
3   www.polcyb.org/ (accessed 25 November 2015).
4   https://twitter.com/mafialand (accessed 25 November 2015).
5   See too his website www.organized-crime.de/oclinx01.htm (accessed 25 November 2015).

9   Conclusions

It is by now abundantly clear that (T)OC (and the related THB) is a serious problem in the contemporary world, and that, far from being in decline, its significance is growing. In this short final chapter, we begin by highlighting the OC patterns identified in this study, before considering factors that are likely to affect its salience in the future. We then produce two scenarios – an optimistic one and a pessimistic one – before drawing overall conclusions.

9.1   Discernible trends

At various points in this book, it has been emphasised that OC is a dynamic phenomenon; what was once true may no longer be so, or may need to be significantly modified. Among the many aspects that have changed in recent decades are:

- OC is much less hierarchically organised and code-based than it used to be; while some of the best-known OC syndicates are still structured in traditional ways, many are not, with flexible networks becoming increasingly common.
- Related to the last point is the fact that some of the best-known traditional OC syndicates have either been essentially destroyed (for example, the major Colombian drug cartels) or are in decline (the Russian thieves-in-law; the Japanese Yakuza; perhaps the Mafia).
- OC has become far more mobile than it was, so that the notion of transnationalisation is more relevant today than ever.
- OC is making ever greater use of technology, especially the Internet, which is used for online scams, identity theft, advertising (drugs; weapons; jobs to entice potential THB victims) and many other relatively new forms of crime.
- Partly as a function of the previous point, OC is making less use of violence than in previous decades; there remain significant

exceptions to this general point, however, with drug cartels having a particularly nasty reputation at present.

- Many OC syndicates are increasingly moving into the legitimate economy, in part as a function of their attempts to launder ill-gotten gains; this in turn means that the line between legal and illegal enterprise is becoming ever more blurred.

- There is also an increasing blurring of the distinction between OC and terrorist organisations. In some cases, the two sides are cooperating more and more with each other, while in others, terrorists are themselves entering what has traditionally been seen as OC's domain, so as to fund their ideological activities. In still other cases – stretching back to the Triads in the nineteenth century – terrorist organisations mutate into OCGs, more concerned with making profit than political statements.

- While not a new trend, it is only since the 1980s that we have fully appreciated that much OC is very small-scale; the Scottish, Australian and Hong Kong government definitions that allow for the use of the term "organised crime" to describe the activities of just two criminals working together highlight this fact.

In addition to these discernible patterns within OC, there are also changing contexts that impact upon the overall OC situation.

9.2   Demographic issues

A problem affecting more and more countries – certainly the more affluent ones – is the greying of the population. As medical knowledge and techniques continue to improve, so people are living longer. Although the retirement age is increasing in some countries, and has been abolished altogether in others, a growing proportion of the population in many states no longer works or else works only part-time. Given that birth rates have fallen in so many countries, with affluent countries again leading the way on this, states need to permit more migrants to make up for the labour shortfalls. But increasing migrant intake is unpopular among sections of the electorate in many countries, with the result that the numbers of migrants are kept relatively low by governing parties so as not to lose support. For precisely the same reason of not wanting to lose support, many opposition parties offer no alternative to this restrictive approach. This mismatch between what is needed and what voters want creates fertile soil for more labour trafficking and people smuggling. Meanwhile, growing affluence in parts of the developing world – the rapid expansion of the middle class – increases demand for designer goods (both real and fake), recreational drugs, online economic activity, and so on, which is good news for OCGs.

9.3   Corruption

Despite some two decades of intense efforts by states, IOs, NGOs and other agencies (for details see Holmes 2015b: 89–126), the global problem of corruption does not appear to be being brought under control. In the press release for its 2014 CPI, Transparency International noted that:

> Corruption is a problem for all economies. . . . More than two thirds of the 175 countries in the 2014 Corruption Perceptions Index score below 50, on a scale from 0 (perceived to be highly corrupt) to 100 (perceived to be very clean). (Transparency International 2014)

In other words, most countries are still quite or very corrupt. The relevance of this to OC is that criminal organisations around the world are able to get away with so much because of the willingness of corrupt officials to collude with them.

9.4   Environmental issues

As noted in Chapter 2, many consider the environment to be the number one global problem of the twenty-first century. In response to this, most states and IOs are seeking to increase environmental protection through greater regulation of activities that impact upon the atmosphere, our flora and fauna, and so on. Unfortunately, the more regulation there is, the more OC will seek to circumvent this to provide products and services that people want, but that have become more difficult or more expensive to obtain through legal channels.

9.5   Communications technology

People everywhere are becoming increasingly dependent on the Internet. As we all make greater use of our tablets, mobile phones, etc. to go online, so we increase our chances of becoming victims of (T)OC.

9.6   The optimistic scenario

The ongoing problems noted above notwithstanding, there are some encouraging signs in the fight against OC. One is that many corporations are now more aware than they once were of the potential impact on sales of negative publicity, and of the legal consequences of being less than rigorous in checking on the sources of particularly cheap products and services. This has encouraged some of them to become more ethical, and to advertise that, for instance, their products are sourced from the fair trade or Anti-Sweatshop movements. While the latter can be traced back to the nineteenth century, it has gained momentum in the era of globalisation, with activists publicly naming and shaming companies such as Nike, Reebok and Wal-Mart for using sweatshops in the developing world, including many that employ child labour, to manufacture their products. This should have a positive impact on the global THB situation, especially vis-à-vis labour trafficking.

While analysing developments in corporate ethics, it is worth noting that some companies are now considering the addition of a fourth line to their annual reports. Since the 1990s, the practice of "triple bottom lining" – in other words, providing the financial accounts bottom line, plus details of what the company has been doing in terms of helping society and the environment, so that another meaning of the "3Ps" (see Chapter 7) is "profit, people and planet" – has spread in the business sector. Firms are now being encouraged to add a fourth bottom line. Quite what this will be is disputed, with some claiming it should be a "culture" or spirituality report on what the company is doing to respect local cultures – traditions, religions, and so on. An alternative view is that the fourth bottom line should be of "governance". Those favouring the latter agree that this additional line should include reporting on what the company is doing to improve transparency, fight corruption and bribery, and so on. In fact, both of these interpretations – culture or governance – focus on the ethical approaches and responsibilities of corporations, and either would thus be a welcome development. The more ethical the licit economy becomes, and the more economically rational it becomes for companies to focus on their social responsibilities, the greater the negative impact this should have on the illicit economy, in which OC plays such a pivotal role.

A third reason for guarded optimism is that authorities around the world have become far more aware of the dangers posed by cybercrime.

While the US has had a Cyber Crimes Center (C3) attached to what is now the Department of Homeland Security (Immigration and Customs Enforcement) since 1997, it was announced in July 2015 that this was to be substantially expanded and upgraded. This, plus the facts that Europol's EC3 commenced work in January 2013, and that Interpol announced in September 2014 its intention to open a cyber-crime centre in Singapore as part of the Interpol Global Complex for Innovation that became operational in 2015, are concrete signs of this recent increased awareness.

In addition to new developments aimed at cybercrime, law enforcement authorities in many countries are making greater use of technology than ever in the fight against OC. For instance, the development of online databases of criminals and criminal activities is making it easier for police agencies to monitor and track OC activity. Another development is the almost exponential growth in the use of CCTV to combat crime of all sorts. Although this has mostly been used to deter street crime, it can also be valuable in detecting and providing evidence on drug dealing, collusion at border crossings, and other aspects of OC activity.

Related to this point about growing use of CCTV is the fact that citizens everywhere are becoming more used to being monitored by the state. Particularly since 9/11, states have been seeking to convince the citizenry that security must often take priority over civil liberties, including the right to privacy. As more countries experience terrorist attacks, so this argument becomes increasingly persuasive, rendering it easier for states to deploy techniques in the fight against OC, such as access to bank accounts and Internet records that would have led to widespread criticism just two decades ago.

At various points in this book, we have emphasised the problems arising from the inability or unwillingness of states to agree on definitions of various types of crime, including OC. The fact that the UNODC has at last – in 2015 – published a draft set of guidelines for standardising definitions should lead to significant improvements in this area in the future. Moreover, agreement on standardised definitions would improve measurement techniques and hence the comparability of data, a useful step forward in the fight against OC.

Many states are increasingly willing to limit some of their own sovereignty. This is already clear in the case of the EU. But it is also evident

– if less advanced – in the development of so many regional organisations, such as the African Union, APEC, ASEAN, Mercosur, NAFTA and the SCO. Although the emphasis in most of these has been on economic cooperation, this can in time lead to cooperation in other fields. This, plus the growing awareness of the impact – including economic – of (T)OC and the often related international terrorism could result in countries that have traditionally been reluctant to conclude extradition treaties becoming more willing to do so.

Finally, it has been demonstrated in this study that a major source of TOC in recent years has been some of the post-communist transition states. Many of these have been consolidating and improving in the 2000s; as this process continues, it is likely that the capacity of the state to deal with OC will increase at the same time as some of the structural drivers – the attraction – of OC will decline.

9.7   The pessimistic scenario

Unfortunately, there are powerful counter currents to those outlined in the optimistic scenario. For instance, while corporations may increasingly produce codes of conduct and in other ways seek to demonstrate to their shareholders and the general public that they are becoming more ethical, one has only to open a newspaper most days of the week to read of the continuing questionable behaviour of so much of the business sector; the 2015 Volkswagen emissions scandal is a major recent example. While corporations profess to care about their reputations for ethical behaviour, it is clear that many are merely paying lip service to this. Companies exist primarily to generate profit; while this has sometimes to be tempered by the equally strong drive to continue to operate into the future, the former tends to dominate the latter when they come into conflict.

Closely connected to this argument is the fact that neo-liberalism and globalisation do not yet appear to have begun to lose their attraction, the GFC notwithstanding. This point is encapsulated well in the title of a 2011 book by Colin Crouch, *The Strange Non-Death of Neoliberalism*. It might have seemed that the GFC would lead people around the world to question whether the global economic system built on neoliberal ideology was flawed, and to see that it had many negative as well as positive consequences. But this did not happen and, as of 2015, it was still showing no signs of emerging, despite the real possibility of another stock market crash and a new global recession. While small numbers of people from Seattle to Europe to Melbourne have been protesting since the 1990s against globalisation and what many of them see as its leading symbols, such as the WTO and the World Economic Forum, the movement has become even smaller. The reasons for this are beyond our remit here. But since neo-liberalism and globalisation were argued in Chapter 6 to be important factors in the rise of TOC, the implications of this "strange non-death" for OC are clear; it assists criminals. In the words of Misha Glenny (2008: 370), "The illegality of labour-smuggling lies in the illogicality of globalisation."

There is no question that globalisation has helped millions of people, and that countries that were once merely developing are now close to being reclassified as developed; China is the most obvious example. But the global economy has been unstable since 2008, and growth rates in many parts of the world – the EU, the US, and now even China – are not as impressive as they once were. The slowdown of an economy often means higher unemployment and a growing sense of (economic) insecurity, which in turn leads some to be attracted to OC as an exit strategy from their deteriorating situation.

A different dimension of the unemployment issue is that some states are ambivalent in their attitudes towards product counterfeiting. For example, while the Chinese authorities mounted operations against factories producing counterfeit goods in 2010–11 and then again in 2012 that have won the praise of the UNODC (Lale-Demoz and Lewis 2013: 124), Beijing also knows that such enterprises help to reduce unemployment, and hence the likelihood of major political unrest. It is possible that China really will clamp down more heavily on counterfeiters, and hence OC, in future – though it might simply outsource some of this production, as it allegedly already has to North Korea (Glenny 2008: 389). Even if China does curtail its (tacit) support for counterfeiting, there are other countries that will step into the vacuum created.

Another discouraging sign is that conflicts are not in decline. As of 2015, the rise of IS in Iraq and Syria, and the ongoing tensions in Ukraine, were just two of the most publicised examples. To the extent that such conflicts increase the demand for irregular migration, this plays into the hands of OC. But conflicts do not only provide OC with new or increased opportunities for people smuggling and the oft-related THB; they also increase demand for illegal weapons and boost post-conflict OCG membership.

Nor are natural disasters going to decline. In fact, given global warming and its knock-on effects (worse flooding, more forest fires, and so on), they will continue to intensify and so further increase the demand for OC to assist with irregular migration.

Sadly, the global demand for illicit drugs is also unlikely to reduce. As the pace of life quickens and our lives become more complex and more pressured, so many will seek relief through recreational drugs, which OC will continue to supply. OC will also continue to supply everyday items that a high percentage of the population in most countries will still opt to purchase at the lowest price possible, whether or not the origin of those cheap goods is suspect.

Despite increased public awareness of the numerous ways in which OC can steal from any one of us via the Internet, and despite the improvements in cyber-security, the fact that Apple Mac software – once considered almost impregnable – has been hacked on various occasions since at least 2012 indicates that cybercriminals are at present still one step ahead of the authorities and the cyber security specialists. There is no compelling reason to assume that this situation will improve.

Finally, the very fact that OC is not as bound by formal borders as states are gives it an advantage over the latter; if demand falls or law enforcement is intensified in one market and country, OC has proven itself very capable of rapidly moving to other markets and jurisdictions.

9.8   The most important factor in the fight against OC

Whether the optimistic or the pessimistic scenario wins out in the future is difficult to predict, though the record to date provides few grounds for assuming it will be the former. However, there is one pair of factors that has been briefly mentioned at various points in this book, and that now has to be elaborated, since it will be the key determining variable.

It is often argued that the single most important factor in the fight against OC is political will. In fact, political will is only a necessary, not a sufficient, condition. In addition to political will, there must be political capacity. All too often, political leaders have sought to address a serious problem, not just OC, only to discover that the people who should be implementing their will, notably state officials, are for whatever reason – it varies by time and place – hindering or even blocking policy implementation. Unless leaderships can secure their staffs' support for the policy, it is likely to remain mere rhetoric.

Even if bureaucrats, police officers and other officers of the state *are* prepared to implement leaderships' policies, there remain two aspects of political will that are crucial. First, are the policies flowing from the political will of the leaders really addressing the issue? In the case of OC, while political leaders can hardly be expected to address psycho-social causes to any meaningful extent, they can often do something about underlying structural (systemic) factors. Making significant changes to economic policy, for example, can reduce unemployment and income inequality, with positive knock-on effects, including on gender inequality. Such changes can reduce the attraction of OC to many marginalised and alienated people, as well as vulnerability to OC deception.

Second, while the political will and the behavioural example of leaders is all-important, it was demonstrated in Chapter 8 that civil society – the business sector, NGOs, the media, and, we can add, religious organisations – all have an important role to play in resisting OC. Finally, each one of us as an individual can play a role – in not using recreational drugs or purchasing suspiciously low-priced goods and services, for instance. In short, everyone's political will matters.

Fighting OC will be an uphill struggle, and while it would be extremely naïve to assume that the war will ever be completely won, many battles can be.

Bibliography

Abadinsky, H. (2013), *Organized Crime* (10th edn), Belmont CA: Wadsworth.

Adelstein, J. (2010), "The last Yakuza", *World Policy Journal*, 27 (2), 63–71.

Adelstein, J. (2012), "The Yakuza lobby", *Foreign Policy (Dispatch)*, 13 December, accessed at http://foreignpolicy.com/2012/12/13/the-yakuza-lobby/ (accessed 8 June 2015).

Agnew, R. (1992), "Foundation for a general strain theory of crime and delinquency", *Criminology*, 30 (1), 47–88.

Albanese, J. and Reichel, P. (eds) (2014), *Transnational Organized Crime*, Thousand Oaks CA: Sage.

Albini, J. (1971), *The American Mafia: Genesis of a Legend*, New York: Appleton-Century-Crofts.

Allum, F. and Gilmour, S. (eds) (2012), *Routledge Handbook of Transnational Organized Crime*, Abingdon: Routledge.

Alvazzi del Frate, A. (2004), "The international crime business survey: findings from nine Central–Eastern European Cities", *European Journal on Criminal Policy and Research*, 10 (2–3), 137–61.

Anderson, S. (2012), "European drug policy: the cases of Portugal, Germany, and the Netherlands", *EUI Political Science Review*, accessed at www.eiu.edu/~polisci/EIU%20Political%20Science%20Review%20Vol%201%20issue%201%20article%202.pdf (accessed 10 August 2015).

Ariely, D. (2008), *Predictably Irrational: The Hidden Forces that Shape Our Decisions*, New York: Harper Collins.

Arsovska, J. (2006), "Understanding a 'culture of violence and crime': the Kanun of Lek Dukagjini and the rise of the Albanian sexual slavery rackets", *European Journal of Crime, Criminal Law and Criminal Justice*, 14 (2), 161–84.

Athanassopoulou, E. (2005), "Fighting organized crime in SEE" in E. Athanassopoulou (ed.), *Fighting Organized Crime in Southeast Europe*, Abingdon: Routledge, pp. 1–6.

Athens, L. (1989), *The Creation of Dangerous Violent Criminals*, London: Routledge.

Athens, L. (1997), *Violent Criminal Acts and Actors Revisited*, Urbana IL: University of Illinois Press.

Australian Crime Commission (2007), *Organised Crime in Australia*, Canberra: Australian Crime Commission.

Baier, C. and Wright, B. (2001), "'If you love me, keep my commandments': a meta-analysis of the effect of religion on crime", *Journal of Research in Crime and Delinquency*, 38 (1), 3–21.

146

Bąkowski, P. (2013a), *The EU Response to Organised Crime*, Brussels: Library of the European Parliament.

Bąkowski, P. (2013b), "Witness protection programmes: EU experiences in the international context", *Library Briefing*, 28 January, Brussels: Library of the European Parliament.

Barker, T. (2014), *Outlaw Motorcycle Gangs as Organized Crime Groups*, New York: Springer.

Bawden, T. (2015), "Food fans are told to prepare for a flood of dangerous counterfeit olive oil", *Independent*, 21 March: 1 and 7.

BBC (2015a), "HSBC bank 'helped clients dodge millions in tax'", *BBC World News*, 10 February, accessed at www.bbc.com/news/business-31248913 (accessed 25 April 2015).

BBC (2015b), "Human trafficking: the lives bought and sold", *BBC World News*, 28 July, accessed at www.bbc.com/news/world-33592634 (accessed 30 July 2015).

BBC One (2008), "Britain's protection racket", *Panorama*, 21 January, at http://news.bbc.co.uk/2/hi/programmes/panorama/7195775.stm (accessed 7 June 2015).

Becker, H. (1963), *Outsiders*, Glencoe IL: Free Press.

Becker, H. (1966), *Outsiders*, New York: Free Press.

Behan, T. (1996), *The Camorra*, London: Routledge.

Bender, J. (2014), "Nearly eight years into the drug war, these are Mexico's 7 most notorious cartels", *Business Insider*, 20 October, accessed at www.businessinsider.com/mexicos-7-most-notorious-drug-cartels-2014-10 (accessed 8 June 2015).

Berry, L., Curtis, G., Elan, S., Hudson, R. and Kollars, N. (2003), *Transnational Activities of Chinese Crime Organizations*, Washington DC: Library of Congress.

Block, A. (1980), *East Side, West Side: Organizing Crime in New York, 1930–1950*, Cardiff: University College Cardiff Press.

Block, A. and Chambliss, W. (1981), *Organizing Crime*, New York: Elsevier.

Block, A. and Scarpitti, F. (1985), *Poisoning for Profit: The Mafia and Toxic Waste in America*, New York: Morrow.

Bocca, R. (2005), "Parla un boss: Così lo Stato pagava la 'ndrangheta per smaltire i rifiuti tossici", *L'Espresso*, 5 August, accessed at www.archivio900.it/it/articoli/art.aspx?r=relauto&id=5978 (accessed 17 August 2015).

Bourdieu, P. (1986), "The forms of capital" in J. Richardson (ed.), *The Handbook of Theory and Research for the Sociology of Education*, New York: Greenwood, pp. 241–58.

Broadhurst, R. (2012), "Black societies and triad-like organized crime in China" in F. Allum and S. Gilmour (eds), *Routledge Handbook of Transnational Organized Crime*, Abingdon: Routledge, pp. 157–70.

Bryan, M., Del Bono, E. and Pudney, S. (2013), *Drug-related Crime*, Colchester: University of Essex.

Business & Human Rights Resource Centre (2014), "US apparel cos. lawsuit (re Saipan)", 18 February, accessed at http://business-humanrights.org/en/us-apparel-cos-lawsuit-re-saipan-0 (accessed 14 April 2015).

Cairncross, F. (1997), *The Death of Distance: How the Communications Revolution Is Changing our Lives*, Cambridge MA: Harvard Business School Press.

Calderoni, F. (2012), "A definition that does not work: the impact of the EU framework decision on the fight against organized crime", *Common Market Law Review*, 49 (4), 1365–93.

Capo (2012), "Mexican drug cartels join forces with Italian Mafia to supply cocaine to Europe", *Mafia Today*, 22 June, accessed at http://mafiatoday.com/tag/mexican-drug-cartels/ (accessed 8 May 2015).

Castells, M. (2010), *End of Millennium – The Information Age: Economy, Society and Culture*, vol. III (2nd edn), Chichester: Wiley-Blackwell.

Chambers, G. (2014), "Charm offensive: Bandidos bikie gang in charity drive for Westmead Children's Hospital", *Daily Telegraph* (Sydney), 28 January.

Chin, K-L. (2014), "Chinese organized crime" in L. Paoli (ed.), *The Oxford Handbook of Organized Crime*, New York: Oxford University Press, pp. 219–33.

Cho, S-Y (2015), "Evaluating policies against human trafficking worldwide: an overview and review of the 3P Index", *Journal of Human Trafficking*, 1 (1), 86–99.

Chu, Y-K, (2000), *Triads as Business*, London: Routledge.

Clarke-Billings, L. (2015), "Child victims of Nepal earthquake sold to factories and brothels by human traffickers", *Independent*, 26 May.

Cloward, R. and Ohlin, L. (1960), *Delinquency and Opportunity*, Glencoe IL: Free Press.

CoE (2013), *Council of Europe Convention on Action against Trafficking in Human Beings*, Strasbourg: Council of Europe.

CoE (2015), "Objectives and mission", accessed at www.coe.int/en/web/sarajevo/objectives-mission (accessed 27 November 2015).

Coleman, J. (1988), "Social capital in the creation of human capital", *American Journal of Sociology*, 94 (Supplement), S95–S120.

Cornish, D. and Clarke, R. (eds) (1986a), *The Reasoning Criminal: Rational Choice Perspectives on Offending*, New York: Springer.

Cornish, D. and Clarke, R. (1986b), "Introduction" in D. Cornish and R. Clarke (eds), *The Reasoning Criminal: Rational Choice Perspectives on Offending*, New York: Springer, pp. 1–16.

Cornish, D. and Clarke, R. (1987), "Understanding crime displacement: an application of rational choice theory", *Criminology*, 25 (4), 933–47.

Council of the European Union (2008), *Council Framework Decision 2008/841/JHA of 24 October 2008 on the fight against organised crime*, accessed at http://eur-lex.europa.eu/legal-content/EN/TXT/?uri=celex:32008F0841 (accessed 24 April 2015).

Cressey, D. (1967), "The functions and structure of criminal syndicates" in US Department of Justice, *Task Force Report: Organized Crime – Annotations and Consultants' Papers*, Washington, DC: US Government Printing Office.

Cressey, D. (1972), *Criminal Organization: Its Elementary Forms*, London: Heinemann.

Cribb, R. (2009), "Introduction: parapolitics, shadow governance and criminal sovereignty" in E. Wilson and T. Lindsey (eds), *Government of the Shadows: Parapolitics and Criminal Sovereignty*, London: Pluto, pp. 1–9.

Crouch, C. (2011), *The Strange Non-Death of Neoliberalism*, Cambridge: Polity.

CSIS (2014), *Net Losses: Estimating the Global Cost of Cybercrime*, Washington DC: Center for Strategic and International Studies.

Curtis, G. (2002), *Involvement of Russian Organized Crime Syndicates, Criminal Elements in the Russian Military, and Regional Terrorist Groups in Narcotics Trafficking in Central Asia, the Caucasus, and Chechnya,* Washington DC: Library of Congress.

Curtis, G. and Karacan, T. (2002), *The Nexus among Terrorists, Narcotics Traffickers, Weapons Proliferators, and Organized Crime Networks in Western Europe,* Washington DC: Library of Congress.

Curtis, G., Elan, S., Hudson, R. and Kollars, N. (2002), "Transnational activities of Chinese crime organizations: a report prepared under an interagency agreement by the Federal Research Division, Library of Congress", *Trends in Organized Crime,* 7 (3), 19–57.

Davidson, P. and Evans, R. (2014), *Poverty in Australia 2014,* Strawberry Hills: Australian Council of Social Service.

Davies, B. (2005), *Black Market,* San Rafael CA: Earth Aware.

Day, M. (2014),"Silvio Berlusconi's links with Italian organised crime confirmed", *Independent,* 12 May.

De Sanctis, F. (2013), *Money Laundering through Art,* Cham: Springer.

Devlin, M. (2010), "Seizing the reform moment: rebuilding Georgia's Police, 2004–2006", *Innovations for Successful Societies,* Princeton University, accessed at http://successfulsocieties.princeton.edu/sites/successfulsocieties/files/Policy_Note_ID126.pdf (accessed 9 June 2013).

Dijk, J. van (2007), "Mafia markers: assessing organized crime and its impact upon societies", *Trends in Organized Crime,* 10 (4), 39–56.

Dijk, J. van (2008), *The World of Crime: Breaking the Silence on Problems of Security, Justice, and Development Across the World,* Thousand Oaks CA: Sage.

Dijk, J. van and Terlouw, G.J. (1996), "An international perspective of the business community as victims of fraud and crime", *Security Journal,* 7 (3), 157–67.

Dorsey, T. and Middleton, P. (n.d.), *Drugs and Crime Facts,* Washington DC: US Department of Justice.

Drug Enforcement Administration (2003), "Massive heroin-smuggling organization dismantled", 16 May, accessed at www.dea.gov/pubs/states/newsrel/2003/nyc051603.html (accessed 12 June 2015).

Dubourg, R. and Prichard, S. (eds) (2006), *Organised Crime: Revenues, Economic and Social Costs, and Criminal Assets Available for Seizure,* London: Home Office.

Dubourg, R. and Prichard, S. (eds) (2007), *The Impact of Organised Crime in the UK: Revenues and Economic and Social Costs,* London: Home Office.

Dugato, M., Favarin, S., Hideg, G. and Illyes, A. (2013), *The Crime Against Businesses in Europe: A Pilot Survey – Final Report,* Brussels: European Commission.

Durkheim, E. (1951), *Suicide: A Study in Sociology,* Glencoe IL: Free Press.

Duyne, P. van (2007), "All in the Dutch construction family: cartel building and organised crime" in L. Holmes (ed.), *Terrorism, Organised Crime and Corruption,* Cheltenham, UK and Northampton MA, USA: Edward Elgar Publishing, pp. 109–29.

Duyne, P. van and Dijck, M. van (2007), "Assessing organised crime: the sad state of an impossible art" in F. Bovenkerk and M. Levi (eds), *The Organised Crime Community: Essays in Honor of Alan A. Block,* New York: Springer, pp. 101–24.

Duyne, P. van, Lampe, K. von and Passas, N. (eds) (2002), *Upperworld and Underworld in Cross-border Crime,* Nijmegen: Wolf.

EBRD (2005), *Transition Report 2005: Business in Transition*, London: European Bank for Reconstruction and Development.

EBRD–World Bank (2005), *Business Environment and Enterprise Performance Survey* (BEEPS), accessed at http://data.worldbank.org/data-catalog/BEEPS (accessed 15 July 2015).

Editorial Board (2015), "Horrors of human trafficking", *New York Times*, 29 May, A22.

EU (2011), "Directive 2011/92/EU of the European Parliament and of the Council of 13 December 2011 on combating the sexual abuse and sexual exploitation of children and child pornography, and replacing Council Framework Decision 2004/68/JHA", *Official Journal of the European Union*, 17 December.

EU (2013), "Directive 2013/40/EU of the European Parliament and of the Council of 12 August 2013 on attacks against information systems and replacing Council Framework Decision 2005/222/JHA", *Official Journal of the European Union*, 14 August.

European Commission (2012), *The EU Strategy towards the Eradication of Trafficking in Human Beings 2012–2016*, Brussels: European Commission.

European Commission (2015), *Daphne Toolkit*, at http://ec.europa.eu/justice/grants/results/daphne-toolkit/ (accessed 13 September 2015).

Europol (2011), *EU Organised Crime Threat Assessment – OCTA 2011*, The Hague: Europol.

Europol (2015), "Europol's priorities", accessed at www.europol.europa.eu/content/page/europol%E2%80%99s-priorities-145 (accessed 27 November 2015).

Eurostat (2015a), *Crime Statistics*, accessed at http://ec.europa.eu/eurostat/statistics-explained/index.php/Crime_statistics (accessed 10 June 2015).

Eurostat (2015b), *Asylum Statistics*, accessed at http://ec.europa.eu/eurostat/statistics-explained/index.php/Asylum_statistics (accessed 12 August 2015).

FATF (2011), *Money Laundering Risks Arising from Trafficking in Human Beings and Smuggling of Migrants*, Paris: FATF/OECD.

FATF (2013), *International Standards on Combating Money Laundering and the Financing of Terrorism and Proliferation*, Paris: FATF/OECD.

FATF (2015), "Money laundering", accessed at www.fatf-gafi.org/pages/faq/moneylaundering/ (accessed 14 March 2015).

FBI (2015), "Glossary of terms", accessed at www.fbi.gov/about-us/investigate/organizedcrime/glossary (accessed 4 June 2015).

Featherstone, L. (2002), *Students against Sweatshops*, New York: Verso.

Featherstone, M. (ed.) (1990), *Global Culture: Nationalism, Globalization and Modernity*, London: Sage.

Fijnaut, C. (2014), "Searching for organized crime in history" in L. Paoli (ed.), *The Oxford Handbook of Organized Crime*, New York: Oxford University Press, pp. 53–95.

Finckenauer, J. (2007), *Mafia and Organized Crime*, London: Oneworld.

Finckenauer, J. and Waring, E. (1998a), *Final Report: Soviet Émigré Organized Criminal Networks in the United States*, accessed at www.ncjrs.gov/pdffiles1/Photocopy/173060NCJRS.pdf (accessed 14 June 2015).

Finckenauer, J. and Waring, E. (1998b), *Russian Mafia in America: Immigration, Culture and Crime*, Boston: Northeastern University Press.

Fisher, N. (1999), "'Workshops of villains': was there much organised crime in classical Athens?" in D. Hopwood (ed.), *Organised Crime in Antiquity*, London: Duckworth and Classical Press of Wales, pp. 53–96.

FLARE (2015), *FLARE Network – Overview*, Turin: Freedom Legality and Rights in Europe.

Fox, S. (1989), *Blood and Power: Organized Crime in 20th Century America*, New York: Morrow.

Freemantle, B. (1995), *The Octopus: Europe in the Grip of Organised Crime*, London: Orion.

Fukuyama, F. (1992), *The End of History and the Last Man*, New York: Free Press.

Fund for Peace (2015), "Fragile States Index", accessed at http://fsi.fundforpeace.org/ (accessed 12 August 2015).

Fyfe, N. and Sheptycki, J. (2005), "Facilitating witness co-operation in organised crime cases: an international review", *Home Office Online Report*, 27/05.

Galeotti, M. (ed.) (2002), *Russian and Post-Soviet Organised Crime*, Aldershot: Ashgate Dartmouth.

Galtung, F. (2006), "Measuring the immeasurable: boundaries and functions of (macro) corruption indices" in C. Sampford, A. Shacklock, C. Connors and F. Galtung (eds), *Measuring Corruption*, Aldershot: Ashgate, pp. 101–30.

Gambetta, D. (1993), *The Sicilian Mafia*, Cambridge MA: Harvard University Press.

Ganev, V. (2001), "The separation of party and state as a logistical problem: a glance at the causes of state weakness in postcommunism", *East European Politics and Societies*, 15 (2), 389–420.

Gecker, J. (2015), "Thai trafficking crackdown targets corrupt police, officials", *New York Times*, 8 May.

Gerth, H. and Wright Mills, C. (eds) (1970), *From Max Weber: Essays in Sociology*, London: Routledge and Kegan Paul.

Giddens, A. (1984), *The Constitution of Society*, Cambridge: Polity.

Gingeras, R. (2014), *Heroin, Organized Crime, and the Making of Modern Turkey*, Oxford: Oxford University Press.

Glenny, M. (2008), *McMafia: Seriously Organised Crime*, London: Bodley Head.

Glenny, M. (2011), *DarkMarket: Cyberthieves, Cybercops and You*, London: Bodley Head.

Gottfredson, M. and Hirschi, T. (1990), *A General Theory of Crime*, Stanford CA: Stanford University Press.

Green, D. and Shapiro, I. (1994), *Pathologies of Rational Choice Theory*, New Haven CT: Yale University Press.

Greenwald, G. (2009), *Drug Decriminalization in Portugal: Lessons for Creating Fair and Successful Drug Policies*, Washington DC: Cato Institute.

Grillo, I. (2011), *El Narco: The Bloody Rise of Mexican Drug Cartels*, London: Bloomsbury.

Guardian (2015), "300 arrested in global wildlife raids", *Guardian*, 19 June.

Hall, T. (2013), "Geographies of the illicit: globalization and organised crime", *Progress in Human Geography*, 37 (3), 366–85.

Harvey, D. (1990), *The Condition of Postmodernity*, Oxford: Blackwell.

Harvey, D. (2005), *A Brief History of Neoliberalism*, Oxford: Oxford University Press.

Hayward, K. and Young, J. (2004), "Cultural criminology: some notes on the script", *Theoretical Criminology*, 8 (3), 259–73.

Hellman, J., Jones, G. and Kaufmann, D. (2000), *Seize the State, Seize the Day: State Capture, Corruption, and Influence in Transition*, Washington DC: World Bank and European Bank of Reconstruction and Development.

Hernández, A. (2013), *Narcoland: The Mexican Drug Lords and Their Godfathers*, London: Verso.

Hess, H. (1998), *Mafia and Mafiosi: Origin, Power and Myth*, London: Hurst.

Hill, C. (2005), "Measuring transnational crime" in P. Reichel (ed.), *Handbook of Transnational Crime and Justice*, Thousand Oaks CA: Sage, pp. 47–65.

Hill, P. (2003), *The Japanese Mafia: Yakuza, Law and the State*, New York: Oxford University Press.

Hill, P. (2014), "The Japanese Yakuza" in L. Paoli (ed.), *The Oxford Handbook of Organized Crime*, New York: Oxford University Press, pp. 234–53.

Hirschi, T. (1969), *Causes of Delinquency*, Berkeley CA: University of California Press.

Hobbs, D. (1998), "Going down the glocal: the local context of organised crime", *Howard Journal of Criminal Justice*, 37 (4), 407–22.

Hobbs, D. and Antonopoulos, G. (2014), "How to research organized crime" in Paoli (2014a), pp. 96–117.

Hobbs, D. and Hobbs, S. (2012), "A bog of conspiracy: the institutional evolution of organized crime in the UK" in F. Allum and S. Gilmour (eds), *Routledge Handbook of Transnational Organized Crime*, Abingdon: Routledge, pp. 250–62.

Hodal, K., Kelly, C. and Lawrence, F. (2014), "Revealed: Asian slave labour producing prawns for supermarkets in US, UK", *Guardian*, 11 June.

Hollersen, W. (2013), "'This Is working': Portugal, 12 years after decriminalizing drugs", *Spiegel Online International*, 27 March.

Holmes, L. (1997), *Post-Communism*, Durham NC: Duke University Press.

Holmes, L. (ed.) (2010a), *Trafficking and Human Rights: European and Asia-Pacific Perspectives*, Cheltenham, UK and Northampton MA, USA: Edward Elgar Publishing.

Holmes, L. (2010b), "Conclusions: quadruple victimisation?" in L. Holmes (ed.), *Trafficking and Human Rights: European and Asia-Pacific Perspectives*, Cheltenham, UK and Northampton MA, USA: Edward Elgar Publishing, pp. 175–205.

Holmes, L. (2014a), "Human trafficking: Asia and Europe" in W. Hofmeister and P. Rueppel (eds), *Trafficking in Human Beings: Learning from Asian and European Experiences*, Singapore: Konrad-Adenauer Stiftung and European Union, pp. 25–38.

Holmes, L. (ed.) (2014b), *Police Corruption: Essential Readings*, Cheltenham, UK and Northampton MA, USA: Edward Elgar Publishing.

Holmes, L. (2015a), "Cybercrime in Russia and CEE" in W. Schreiber and M. Kosienkowski (eds), *Digital Eastern Europe*, Wroclaw: KEW, 2015, Kindle e-book, locs 814–1179.

Holmes, L. (2015b), *Corruption: A Very Short Introduction*, Oxford: Oxford University Press.

Hong Kong Government (2014), *Chapter 455 – Organized and Serious Crimes Ordinance*, Hong Kong: Hong Kong Government.

Hopwood, D. (ed.) (1999), *Organised Crime in Antiquity*, London: Duckworth and Classical Press of Wales.

Hough, P. (2011), "Guerrilla insurgency as organized crime: explaining the so-called "political involution" of the Revolutionary Armed Forces of Colombia", *Politics and Society*, 39 (3), 379–414.

Howe, C. (2005), "Non-discriminatory approaches to address clients in prostitution" in A. Erdelmann, K. Brunner, A. Niehaus and J. Willems (eds) (2005), *Challenging Trafficking in Persons: Theoretical Debate and Practical Approaches*, Baden-Baden: Nomos, pp. 98–103.

Hughes, C., Ritter, A., Cowdery, N. and Phillips, B. (2014), "Australian threshold quantities for "drug trafficking": are they placing drug users at risk of unjustified sanction?", *Trends and Issues in Criminal Justice*, 467, 1–7.

Hutchinson, S. and O'Malley, P. (2007), "A crime–terror nexus? Thinking on some of the links between terrorism and criminality", *Studies in Conflict Terrorism*, 30 (2), 1095–107.

ICIJ (2014), "Luxemburg leaks: global companies' secrets exposed", accessed at www.icij.org/project/luxembourg-leaks (accessed 25 April 2015).

ILO (2001), *The Director-General's Programme and Budget Proposals for 2002–03*, Geneva: International Labour Office.

Interpol (2014), *Pharmaceutical Crime and Organized Criminal Groups*, Lyon: Interpol.

Interpol (2015), "Money laundering", accessed at www.interpol.int/Crime-areas/Financial-crime/Money-laundering (accessed 24 April 2015).

IOM (2004), *IOM Counter-Trafficking Activities*, Geneva: International Organization for Migration.

Jamieson, A. (1995), "The transnational dimension of Italian organized crime", *Transnational Organized Crime*, 1 (2), 151–72.

Kaplan, D. and Dubro, A. (2012), *Yakuza: Japan's Criminal Underworld*, Berkeley CA: University of California Press.

Kartha, T. (2000), "Organised crime and the illegal market in weapons in Southern Asia", *Strategic Analysis*, 24 (2), 403–22.

Kelly, A. (2014), "Supermarket giants in Thailand for prawn slavery talks", *Guardian*, 30 July.

Kelly, A. and McNamara, M-L. (2015), "3,000 children enslaved in Britain after being trafficked from Vietnam", *Guardian*, 24 May.

Kington, T. (2007), "From cocaine to plutonium: mafia clan accused of trafficking nuclear waste", *Guardian*, 9 October.

Kleemans, E. (2014), "Theoretical perspectives on organized crime" in Paoli (2014a), pp. 32–52.

Krebs, B. (2014), *Spam Nation*, Naperville IL: Sourcebooks.

Lale-Demoz, A. and Lewis, G. (eds) (2013), *Transnational Organized Crime in East Asia and the Pacific: A Threat Assessment*, Bangkok: United Nations Office on Drugs and Crime.

Lampe, K. von (2001), "Not a process of enlightenment: the conceptual history of organized crime in Germany and the United States of America", *Forum on Crime and Society*, 1 (2), 99–116.

Lampe, K. von (2004), "Measuring organised crime: a critique of current approaches" in P. van Duyne, M. Jager, K. von Lampe and J. Newell (eds), *Threats and Phantoms of Organised Crime, Corruption and Terrorism*, Nijmegen: Wolf Legal Publishers, pp. 85–116.

Lampe, K. von (2005), "Making the second step before the first: assessing organized crime – the case of Germany", *Crime, Law and Social Change*, 42 (4–5), 227–59.

Lauchs, M., Bain, A. and Bell, P. (2015), *Outlaw Motorcycle Gangs: A Theoretical Perspective*, Basingstoke: Palgrave Macmillan.

Lawrence, F. (2012), "Workers who collected Freedom Food chickens 'were trafficked and beaten'", *Guardian*, 29 October.

Lawrence, F. (2015), "Lithuanian migrants trafficked to UK egg farms sue 'worst gang-master ever'", *Guardian*, 10 August.

Leitzel, J. (1995), *Russian Economic Reform*, London: Routledge.

Lemert, E. (1951), *Social Pathology: A Systematic Approach to the Theory of Sociopathic Behavior*, New York: McGraw Hill.

Levi, M., Innes, M., Reuter, P. and Gundur, R. (2013), *The Economic, Financial and Social Impacts of Organised Crime in the European Union*, Brussels: European Union.

Levitt, S. and Dubner, S. (2005), *Freakonomics*, New York: Morrow.

Libera (2015), "Libera: Associazioni, nomi e numeri contro le mafie", accessed at www.libera.it/flex/cm/pages/ServeBLOB.php/L/IT/IDPagina/70 (accessed 27 November 2015).

Lichbach, M. (2003), *Is Rational Choice Theory All of Social Science?*, Ann Arbor MI: University of Michigan Press.

Lintner, B. (2002), *Blood Brothers: Crime, Business and Politics in Asia*, Crows Nest, NSW: Allen and Unwin.

Lo, S. (2008), *The Politics of Cross-border Crime in Greater China: Case Studies of Mainland China, Hong Kong, and Macao*, Armonk: M.E. Sharpe.

Lunde, P. (2004), *Organized Crime: An Inside Guide to the World's Most Successful Industry*, New York: DK [Dorling Kindersley].

Lyman, M. and Potter, G. (2015), *Organized Crime* (6th edn), Boston: Pearson.

Marsden, W. and Sher, J. (2006), *Angels of Death*, London: Hodder and Stoughton.

Martin, G. (2014), "Terrorism and transnational organized crime" in J. Albanese and P. Reichel (eds), *Transnational Organized Crime: An Overview from Six Continents*, Thousand Oaks CA: Sage, pp. 163–93.

Mason, T.D. and Galbreath, D. (2004), "Ethnicity and politics" in M. Hawkesworth and M. Kogan (eds), *Encyclopedia of Government and Politics*, vol. 1 (2nd edn), London: Routledge, pp. 542–75.

McCarthy, D. (2011), *An Economic History of Organized Crime: A National and Transnational Approach*, Abingdon: Routledge.

McLuhan, M. (1962), *The Gutenberg Galaxy: The Making of Typographic Man*, Toronto: University of Toronto Press.

McLuhan, M. (1964), *Understanding Media: The Extensions of Man*, New York: McGraw-Hill.

McQuade, A. (2015), "Human traffickers are targeting Nepal – we must do more to help", *Guardian*, 7 May.

Meacham, C. (2014), "Capturing Public Enemy No. 1", *CNN online*, 23 February, accessed at http://edition.cnn.com/2014/02/23/opinion/meacham-cartel-boss-arrest/ (accessed 4 August 2014).

Medel, M. and Thoumi, F. (2014), "Mexican drug 'cartels'" in L. Paoli (ed.), *The Oxford Handbook of Organized Crime*, New York: Oxford University Press, pp. 196–218.

Merton, R. (1938), "Social structure and anomie", *American Sociological Review*, 3 (5), 672–82.

Meyer, S. (2006), "Trafficking in human organs in Europe: a myth or an actual threat?", *European Journal of Crime, Criminal Law and Criminal Justice*, 14 (2), 208–29.

Michaletos, I. (2007), "Shape of the Albanian organized crime", *Research Institute for European and American Studies*, 25 July, accessed at www.rieas.gr/research-areas/terrorism-studies/327-shape-of-the-albanian-organized-crime (accessed 24 August 2015).

Michaletos, I. (2012), "Southeastern European organized crime and extremism review", *Serbianna*, 26 November, accessed at http://serbianna.com/analysis/archives/1706 (accessed 14 April 2015).

Michaletos, I. and Markos, S. (2007), "Albania and EUROPOL sign agreement on organized crime", *Worldpress.org*, 7 March, accessed at www.worldpress.org/Europe/2705.cfm (accessed 7 May 2014).

Miller, W. B. (1958), "Lower class culture as a generating milieu of gang delinquency", *Journal of Social Issues*, 14 (3), 5–19.

Miró, R. (2003), *Organized Crime and Terrorist Activity in Mexico 1999–2002*, Washington DC: Library of Congress.

Morselli, C. (2005), *Contacts, Opportunities, and Criminal Enterprise*, Toronto: University of Toronto Press.

Morselli, C. (2010), *Inside Criminal Networks*, New York: Springer.

Morselli, C. (ed.) (2014), *Crime and Networks*, New York: Routledge.

Munck, R. (2010), "Slavery: exception or rule?" in G. Wylie and P. McRedmond (eds), *Human Trafficking in Europe: Character, Causes and Consequences*, Basingstoke: Palgrave Macmillan, pp. 17–29.

Murphy, C. (2015), "Sex workers' rights are human rights", *Amnesty International*, 14 August, accessed at www.amnesty.org/en/latest/news/2015/08/sex-workers-rights-are-human-rights/ (accessed 18 September 2015).

Naím. M. (2003), "The five wars of globalization", *Foreign Policy*, 134, 28–37.

National Security Council (2011), *Transnational Organized Crime: A Growing Threat to National and International Security*, accessed at www.whitehouse.gov/administration/eop/nsc/transnational-crime/threat (accessed 6 June 2015).

Naylor, R.T. (1993), "The insurgent economy: black market operations of guerrilla organizations", *Crime, Law and Social Change*, 20 (1), 13–51.

Naylor, R.T. (1995), "From Cold War to Crime War: The Search for a New 'National Security' Threat", *Transnational Organized Crime*, 1 (4), 37–56.

Naylor, R.T. (1997), "Mafias, myths and markets: on the theory and practice of enterprise crime", *Transnational Organized Crime*, 3 (3), 13–43.

Naylor, R.T. (2002), *Wages of Crime: Black Markets, Illegal Finance, and the Underworld Economy*, Ithaca NY: Cornell University Press.

NCA (2014), *National Strategic Assessment of Serious and Organised Crime 2014*, London: National Crime Agency.

NCA (2015), *National Strategic Assessment of Serious and Organised Crime 2015*, London: National Crime Agency.

NCPC (2015), "Intellectual property theft: get real", accessed at www.ncpc.org/topics/intellectual-property-theft/gangs-and-organized-crime-1 (accessed 3 June 2015).

Nellemann, C. and Interpol Environmental Crime Programme (eds) (2012), *Green Carbon, Black Trade: Illegal Logging, Tax Fraud and Laundering in the World's Tropical Forests*, Arendal: United Nations Environment Programme and GRID-Arendal.

Nuzzi, G. and Antonelli, C. (2012), *Blood Ties: The 'Ndrangheta – Italy's New Mafia*, London: Pan Macmillan.

O'Brien, M. (2005), "What is *cultural* about cultural criminology?", *British Journal of Criminology*, 45 (5), 599–612.

Ohmae, K. (1990), *The Borderless World: Power and Strategy in the Interlinked Economy*, New York: Harper Business.

Orenstein, R. (2013), *Ivory, Horn and Blood*, Richmond Hill ON: Firefly.

Organized Crime Research (2015), "A tribute to Donald R. Cressey (1919–1987)", accessed at www.organized-crime.de/cressey.htm (accessed 14 April 2015).

OSCE (2010), *Unprotected Work, Invisible Exploitation: Trafficking for the Purpose of Domestic Servitude*, Vienna: OSCE.

PACO (2002), *Trafficking in Human Beings and Corruption: Report on the Regional Seminar*, Strasbourg: Council of Europe.

Paoli, L. (ed.) (2014a), *The Oxford Handbook of Organized Crime*, New York: Oxford University Press.

Paoli, L. (2014b), "The Italian Mafia" in L. Paoli (ed.), *The Oxford Handbook of Organized Crime*, New York: Oxford University Press, pp. 121–41.

Paoli, L. and Vander Beken, T. (2014), "Organized crime: a contested concept" in Paoli (2014a), pp. 13–31.

Patrick, S. (2006), "Weak states and global threats: fact or fiction?", *The Washington Quarterly*, 29 (2), 27–53.

Penglase R.B. (2005), "The shutdown of Rio de Janeiro: the poetics of drug trafficker violence", *Anthropology Today*, 21 (5), 3–6.

Platt, S. (2015), *Criminal Capital: How the Finance Industry Facilitates Crime*, Basingstoke: Palgrave Macmillan.

Plywaczewski, E. (2002), "Chinese organized crime in Western and Eastern Europe", paper delivered to 3rd annual symposium on "Crime and Its Control in Greater China", 21–22 June, accessed at http://usinfo/state.gov/regional/ea/chinaaliens/polishprof.htm (accessed 17 April 2013).

Poznanski, K. (1992), "Epilogue: markets and states in the transformation of post-communist Europe" in K. Poznanski (ed.), *Constructing Capitalism: The Reemergence of Civil Society and Liberal Economy in the Post-Communist World*, Boulder CO: Westview, pp. 199–219.

Putnam, R. (1993), *Making Democracy Work: Civic Traditions in Modern Italy*, Princeton NJ: Princeton University Press.

Rademeyer, J. (2012), *Killing for Profit*, Cape Town: Random House Struik.

Ramsey, G. (2011), "Poverty a recruitment tool for Mexico's criminal gangs", *Insight Crime*, 20 July, accessed at www.insightcrime.org/news-analysis/poverty-a-recruit ment-tool-for-mexicos-criminal-gangs (accessed 17 August 2015).

Rankin, A. (2012), "Recent trends in organized crime in Japan: Yakuza vs. the police, and foreign crime gangs – Part 2", *Asia Pacific Journal – Japan Focus*, 8, accessed at www. japanfocus.org/-Andrew-Rankin/3692/article.pdf (accessed 28 July 2015).

Rawlinson, P. (1997), "Russian organised crime: a brief history" in Williams (1997a), pp. 28–52.

Reuter, P. (1983), *Disorganized Crime*, Cambridge MA: MIT Press.

Reuter, P. (1994), "Research on American organized crime" in R. Kelly, K.-L. Chin and R. Schatzberg (eds), *Handbook of Organized Crime in the United States*, Westport CT: Greenwood Press, pp. 91–120.

Rogowski, R. and Wasserspring, L. (1971), *Does Political Development Exist? Corporatism in Old and New Societies*, Beverley Hills CA: Sage.

Rojkov, A. (2015), "Die Mütter des Menschenhandels", *Frankfurter Allgemeine Zeitung*, 30 March.

Ruggiero, V. (1996), *Organised and Corporate Crime in Europe: Offers That Can't Be Refused*, Aldershot: Dartmouth.

Saisana, M. and Saltelli, A. (2012), *Corruption Perceptions Index 2012: Statistical Assessment*, Luxembourg: European Union.

Sanderson, T. (2004), "Transnational terror and organized crime: blurring the lines", *SAIS Review*, 24 (1), 49–61.

Saviano, R. (2007), *Gomorrah: Italy's Other Mafia*, New York: Farrar, Straus and Giroux.

Schelling, T. (1971), "What is the business of organized crime?", *The American Scholar*, 40 (4), 643–52.

Schori Liang, C. (2011), "Shadow networks: the growing nexus of terrorism and organised crime", *GCSP Policy Paper*, No. 20, Geneva: Geneva Centre for Security Policy.

Schram, P. and Tibbetts, S. (2014), *Introduction to Criminology*, Thousand Oaks CA: Sage.

Schulte-Bockholt, A. (2006), *The Politics of Organized Crime and the Organized Crime of Politics*, Oxford: Lexington.

Schwab, K. (ed.) (2010), *The Global Competitiveness Report 2010/11*, Geneva: World Economic Forum.

Schwab, K. (ed.) (2014), *The Global Competitiveness Report 2014/15*, Geneva: World Economic Forum.

Sellin, T. (1938), "Culture conflict and crime", *American Journal of Sociology*, 44 (1), 97–103.

Serenata, N. (ed.) (2014), *The 'Ndrangheta and Sacra Corona Unita: The History, Organization and Operations of Two Unknown Mafia Groups*, Cham: Springer.

Serio, J. (2008), *Investigating the Russian Mafia*, Durham NC: Carolina Academic Press.

Serious Organised Crime Taskforce (2009), *Letting Our Communities Flourish: A Strategy for Tackling Serious Organised Crime in Scotland*, Edinburgh: Scottish Government.

Shelley, L. (2003), "Trafficking in women: the business model approach", *Brown Journal of World Affairs*, 10 (1), 119–31.

Shelley, L. and Picarelli (2005), "Methods and motives: exploring links between transnational organized crime and international terrorism", *Trends in Organized Crime*, 9 (2), 52–67.

Siegel, D. and Bunt, H. van de (eds) (2012), *Traditional Organized Crime in the Modern World: Responses to Socioeconomic Change*, New York: Springer.

Siegel, D. and Nelen, H. (2008), "Introduction" in D. Siegel and H. Nelen (eds), *Organized Crime: Culture, Markets and Policies*, New York: Springer, pp. 1–3.

Silvester, J. (2015), "International bikie gangs target Victoria for business", *The Age*, 16 March, 1 and 7.

Smith, C., Rush, J. and Burton, C. (2013), "Street gangs, organized crime groups, and terrorists: differentiating criminal organizations", *Investigative Sciences Journal*, 5 (1), 1–18.

Smith, D. (1975), *The Mafia Mystique*, New York: Basic.

Smith, D. (1980), "Paragons, pariahs, and pirates: a spectrum-based theory of enterprise", *Crime and Delinquency*, 26 (3), 358–86.

Steger, M. (2013), *Globalization: A Very Short Introduction*, Oxford: Oxford University Press.

Sterling, C. (1994), *Thieves World: The Threat of the New Global Network of Organized Crime*, New York: Simon and Shuster; also published as *Crime Without Frontiers: The Worldwide Expansion of Organized Crime and the Pax Mafiosa*, New York: Little Brown.

Stiglitz, J. (2002), *Globalization and its Discontents*, London: Penguin.

Talalayev, G. (1993), "Boris Yeltsin addresses all-Russia conference on problems of the fight against organized crime and corruption: full text of speech", *ITAR-TASS*, 12 February.

Tannenbaum, F. (1938), *Crime and the Community*, New York: Columbia University Press.

Territo, L. and Matteson, R. (eds) (2012), *The International Trafficking of Human Organs: A Multidisciplinary Perspective*, Boca Raton FL: CRC Press.

Thompson, K. and Jernow, A. (2008), *Compensation for Trafficked and Exploited Persons in the OSCE Region*, Warsaw: OSCE Office for Democratic Institutions and Human Rights.

Tiffen, R. (1999), *Scandals, Media and Corruption in Contemporary Australia*, Sydney: University of New South Wales Press.

Tilly, C. (1985), "War making and state making as organized crime" in P. Evans, D. Rueschemeyer and T. Skocpol (eds), *Bringing the State Back In*, Cambridge: Cambridge University Press, pp. 169–91.

Transparency International (2014), "Corruption Perceptions Index 2014: Clean Growth at Risk", accessed at www.transparency.org/cpi2014/press (accessed 27 November 2015).

Transparency International (2015), *Corruption Perceptions Index – Overview*, accessed at www.transparency.org/research/cpi/overview (accessed 15 August 2015).

Travis, A. (2014), "UK firms to face new rules aimed at ending slavery in supply chains", *Guardian*, 13 October.

Trevaskes, S. (2010), *Policing Serious Crime in China: From "Strike Hard" to "Kill Fewer"*, Abingdon: Routledge.

Tusikov, N. (2012), "Measuring organised crime-related harms: exploring five policing methods", *Crime, Law and Social Change*, 57 (1), 99–115.

UNAMA (2015), "UN Security Council Committee Report indicates Taliban strengthening links to organized crime", accessed at http://unama.unmissions.org/Default.aspx?ctl=Details&tabid=12254&mid=15756&ItemID=38567 (accessed 12 June 2015).

UNHCR (2013), *Asylum Trends 2012*, Geneva: UNHCR.

UNIAP (2009), *International Trafficking in Persons Laws*, United Nations Inter-Agency Project on Human Trafficking, accessed at www.no-trafficking.org/resources_int_tip_laws.html (accessed 25 April 2015).

UNODC (2004), *United Nations Convention against Transnational Organized Crime and the Protocols Thereto*, New York: United Nations.

UNODC (2010), *The Globalization of Crime: A Transnational Organised Crime Threat Assessment*, Vienna: United Nations Office on Drugs and Crime.

UNODC (2011a), *Estimating Illicit Financial Flows Resulting from Drug Trafficking and Other Transnational Organized Crimes*, Vienna: United Nations Office on Drugs and Crime.

UNODC (2011b), *Issue Paper: The Role of Corruption in Trafficking in Persons*, Vienna: United Nations.

UNODC (2012), *Digest of Organized Crime Cases*, New York: United Nations.

UNODC (2014), *Global Report on Trafficking in Persons 2014*, New York: United Nations.

UNODC (2015a), *International Classification of Crime for Statistical Purposes (ICCS), Version 1.0*, Vienna: United Nations Office on Drugs and Crime.

UNODC (2015b), "United Nations Convention against Transnational Organized Crime and the protocols thereto", accessed at www.unodc.org/unodc/treaties/CTOC/ (accessed 27 November 2015).

UNODC (2015c), "About UNODC", accessed at www.unodc.org/unodc/en/about-unodc/index.html?ref=menutop (accessed 27 November 2015).

UNODC (2015d), "UNODC on human trafficking and migrant smuggling", accessed at www.unodc.org/unodc/en/human-trafficking/ (accessed 27 November 2015).

UNODC/UNECE Task Force on Crime Classification (2012), *Principles and Framework for an International Classification of Crimes for Statistical Purposes*, Vienna and Geneva: United Nations Office on Drugs and Crime and United Nations Economic Commission for Europe.

US Department of State (2007), *Trafficking in Persons Report 2007*, Washington DC: US Department of State.

US Department of State (2014), *Trafficking in Persons Report 2014*, Washington DC: US Department of State.

US Department of State (2015), *Trafficking in Persons Report 2015*, Washington DC: US Department of State.

Vander Beken, T. (2004), "Risky business: a risk-based methodology to measure organized crime", *Crime, Law and Social Change*, 41 (5), 471–516.

Vander Beken, T. et al. (2006), *Measuring Organised Crime in Europe: A Feasibility*

Study of a Risk-Based Methodology across the European Union, Antwerp-Apeldoorn: Maklu.

Varese, F. (2001), *The Russian Mafia: Private Protection in a New Market Economy*, Oxford: Oxford University Press.

Veno, A. (2009), *The Brotherhoods: Inside the Outlaw Motorcycle Clubs*, Crows Nest: Allen and Unwin.

Vines, S. (1998), "Chinese rule boosts Hong Kong triads", *Independent*, 22 March.

Volkov, V. (2014), "The Russian Mafia: rise and extinction" in L. Paoli (ed.), *The Oxford Handbook of Organized Crime*, New York: Oxford University Press, pp. 159–76.

Webster, W. (ed.) (1997), *Russian Organized Crime: Global Organized Crime Project*, Washington DC: Center for Strategic and International Studies.

Wees, H. van (1999), "The Mafia of early Greece: violent exploitation in the seventh and sixth centuries BC" in D. Hopwood (ed.), *Organised Crime in Antiquity*, London: Duckworth and Classical Press of Wales, pp. 1–51.

Williams, P. (ed.) (1997a), *Russian Organized Crime: The New Threat?*, London: Cass.

Williams, P. (1997b), "Introduction: how serious a threat is Russian organized crime?" in P. Williams (ed.), *Russian Organized Crime: The New Threat?* London: Cass, pp. 1–27.

Williams, P. (2001), "Crime, illicit markets, and money laundering" in P. J. Simmons and C. de Jonge Oudraat (eds), *Managing Global Issues: Lessons Learned*, Washington DC: Carnegie Endowment for International Peace, pp. 106–50.

Williams, R. (1976), *Keywords: A Vocabulary of Culture and Society*, London: Fontana/Croom Helm.

Wilson, E. and Lindsey, T. (eds) (2009), *Government of the Shadows: Parapolitics and Criminal Sovereignty*, London: Pluto.

Wilson, S. (2014), "Mexico arrests 32 policemen for alleged organised crime ties", *Telegraph*, 28 July.

Woodfall, D. (2007), "From cocaine to plutonium: mafia clan accused of trafficking nuclear waste", *Guardian*, 9 October.

World Bank (2009), *What are the Cross-Cutting Themes?*, accessed at http://web.worldbank.org/archive/website01020/WEB/0__CON-8.HTM (accessed 17 August 2015).

World Bank (2014), "Unemployment, total (% of total labor force) (modeled ILO estimate)", accessed at http://data.worldbank.org/indicator/SL.UEM.TOTL.ZS (accessed 25 February 2015).

World Bank (2015), "GINI index (World Bank estimate)", accessed at http://data.worldbank.org/indicator/SI.POV.GINI?page=3 (accessed 14 June 2015).

Wren, C. (1998), "Drugs or alcohol linked to 80% of inmates", *New York Times*, 9 January, accessed at www.nytimes.com/1998/01/09/us/drugs-or-alcohol-linked-to-80-of-inmates.html (accessed 5 March 2015).

Wright, A. (2006), *Organised Crime*, Cullompton: Willan.

Wyatt, T. (2013), *Wildlife Trafficking: A Deconstruction of the Crime, the Victims, and the Offenders*, Basingstoke: Palgrave Macmillan.

Yen, I. (2008), "Of vice and men: a new approach to eradicating sex trafficking by reducing male demand through educational programs and abolitionist legislation", *Journal of Criminal Law and Criminology*, 98 (2), 653–86.

Zoutendijk, A. (2010), "Organised crime threat assessments: a critical review", *Crime, Law and Social Change*, 54 (1), 63–86.

Zuckerman, P. (2009), "Atheism, secularity, and well-being: how the findings of social science counter negative stereotypes and assumptions", *Sociology Compass*, 3 (6), 949–71.

Index